Shaky Ground

DEBATES IN ARCHAEOLOGY

Series editor: Richard Hodges

Shaky Ground

Context, Connoisseurship and the History of Roman Art

Elizabeth Marlowe

B L O O M S B U R Y

LONDON • NEW DELHI • NEW YORK • SYDNEY

Bloomsbury Academic

An imprint of Bloomsbury Publishing Plc

50 Bedford Square	1385 Broadway
London	New York
WC1B 3DP	NY 10018
UK	USA

www.bloomsbury.com

Bloomsbury is a registered trade mark of Bloomsbury Publishing Plc

First published 2013

British Library Cataloguing-in-Publication Data
A catalogue record for this book is available from the British Library.

ISBN: HB: 978-0-71564-064-7
ePub: 978-1-47250-2094
ePDF: 978-1-47250-2100

Library of Congress Cataloging-in-Publication Data
A catalog record for this book is available from the Library of Congress.

Typeset by Fakenham Prepress Solutions, Fakenham, Norfolk NR21 8NN
Printed and bound in Great Britain

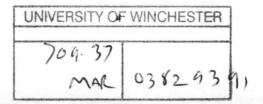

Contents

Acknowledgments

The research for this book was supported by generous grants from the Colgate University Research Council, including a Picker grant that made the travel possible. I am grateful to my Colgate colleagues in Art and Art History, especially my patient and perceptive chair, Bob McVaugh, for the many ways, large and small, that they have encouraged this project. My Colgate students have also been a nourishing source of energy, curiosity and inspiration, particularly Claudia Piacente, Jeremy Rhodes, Eliza Graham, Ashlee Eve, and Frances Kahan. Nicole Beletsky and Elizabeth Johnson have served as reliable, competent research assistants.

For various forms of expertise and assistance, I am grateful to Fabio Barry, Dorian Borbonus, Robert Cohon, Joseph Connors, Sophie Descamps, Steven Ellis, Jasper Gaunt, David Gill, Juliet Istrabadi, Christine Kondoleon, Ken Lapatin, Christopher Lightfoot, Peter Lukehart, John Moore, Timothy Motz, Oscar White Muscarella, Carole Paul, Victoria Reed, Peter Rockwell, and Julie Van Voorhis.

Audiences and gracious hosts at the Roman Archaeology Conference in 2008, the Smith College Museum Studies Program, the Syracuse chapter of the Archaeological Institute of America, Middlebury College, Skidmore College and the Center for Heritage and Society at the University of Massachusetts Amherst asked thoughtful questions that sharpened my thinking and sometimes changed my mind. Friends and colleagues have done so as well, including Dan Bouk, Patrick Crowley, Lesleigh Cushing, Noah Dauber, Jane Fejfer, Eliza Garrison, Elaine Gazda, Andrew Gordon, Michael Koortbojian, Laura Lesswing and Joshua Shannon.

There has been nothing more useful and pleasurable than discussing these ideas in front of objects in museums in the company of critically perceptive friends, and for that privilege I am deeply indebted to Padma Kaimal, Johanna Blokker, Ashli Baker, Susanna McFadden,

Rebecca Molholt, Barbara Kellum and Ken Lapatin. Ashli Baker gets special props for her fearless Turkish driving. Thanks also to Lisa Fentress, who made my many stays in Rome comfortable and stimulating; and to my sister and her husband, Nancy and Andrew Gordon, for doing the same in New York, and for Nancy's eagle-eyed proofreading and last minute photography.

My Columbia University advisor, Richard Brilliant, has been patient, generous and supportive—even if he is somewhat skeptical of this particular project. It is a profound source of sadness not to be able to thank in person my other graduate school mentor, Tally Kampen, for all the ways she pushed me over the years, and a deep source of regret not to have taken better advantage of her innovative thinking about Roman provincial art while I had the chance. She is much missed.

More than anything, this book is a product of conversations carried on over the past fifteen years with the members of the "Pioneer Valley Roman Forum," an informal group that has been convening at various locations between Mt. Holyoke and New York City and sharing work in progress. There have been too many thoughtful, challenging interlocutors from that community over the years to name them all, but Rebecca Molholt, Jim Frakes, Barbara Kellum and Bettina Bergmann in particular have been consummate mentor-friends, challenging and encouraging. They also offered insightful and incisive comments on the manuscript, as did Ken Lapatin and Patrick Crowley.

My biggest debt of gratitude is to my husband, Robert Nemes, who inspires me to be a better thinker and a better person, and who supports my efforts to do so in every conceivable way; and to our two delightful daughters, Arielle and Dahlia, for whom one of my greatest hopes is that someday they will find as much stimulation in their work as I have found in thinking and talking through the ideas presented here.

List of Figures

All photos by author unless otherwise noted.

Introduction: Contradictions

Grounded and ungrounded

A few years ago, I taught a seminar for art history majors at my college called "Looting, Faking, Collecting and Understanding Antiquities in the Post-Colonial World." We read about the trials of antiquities traffickers in Italy, the Elgin Marbles, the UNESCO Convention of 1970, the concept of the "universal museum," forgeries and connoisseurship. We visited the Metropolitan Museum of Art, some Madison Avenue galleries, and the home of a private collector. Discussions in class were lively and occasionally heated, but frequently circled back to the necessarily different ways of knowing ancient artworks that do and don't have a documented findspot. For their research papers, each student was assigned an archaeologically-undocumented bronze statuette in our college art museum. They appreciated the objects' beauty, analyzed their forms, and compared them to other works with similar forms. But they quickly realized the degree to which the statuettes' lack of ancient context limited the questions they could ask about them, wondering fruitlessly where and with what other objects these were originally displayed, who might have seen them, what their larger social significance might have been. The students were also shocked to learn that the authenticity of the statuettes was not a matter of complete certainty.

Meanwhile, in the lower-level Roman Art survey course I was also teaching that semester, I was cheerfully reaching for the canonical images I'd always reached for when teaching that course, the same images I had been shown as a student, the same ones featured in all the standard survey textbooks. When seeking to explain the function of private portraiture in the Roman world, I naturally chose the Barberini Togatus; when the topic was ideal female beauty, the obvious choice was the Fonseca bust (aka the "Flavian Beauty") in the Capitoline Museum; for the militaristic imperial ideal of the third century, the scowling portraits of Caracalla and Trebonianus Gallus at the Metropolitan Museum, and so on.

Eventually, however, the contradictions between the two courses became impossible to ignore. Very few of those canonical works of Roman art—the ones that serve as the bedrock and baseline of the entire discipline—have come down to us with a known findspot. Indeed, somewhere between one-third and one-half of all the free-standing sculpture in the Roman art surveys has no reliable data about its ancient setting (the amount is closer to 75 percent for the sculpture in the Roman chapters of introductory textbooks such as Janson and Stokstad). The oft-repeated platitudes about such works' meanings—in the cases of those just mentioned, the veneration of ancestors, the vanity of aristocratic women, and the brutishness of the soldier-emperors—are not the product of any real knowledge about those particular objects' ancient patrons or users. They are derived, rather, from literary texts (Cicero, Juvenal, and the authors of the *Historia Augusta*, respectively), which have been used to fill in the historical gaps left by these artworks' missing ancient contexts. Their fame is due not to the richness of their historical documentation, but to their beauty, exceptional state of preservation, and prominence in the best-known collections. Indeed, so great is their celebrity that the fact of their unknown archaeological origins is scarcely mentioned in either the textbooks or in more scholarly publications. I had certainly never drawn attention to it in my teaching.

Despite the ostensible shift toward "social art history" more than a generation ago, indifference to context remains ingrained in much of Roman art history today. This book attempts to show how that is so and why it is a problem. It advocates three basic practices: the full and consistent itemization of both findspot data and ownership history of all works discussed (much as name, date, material, and present whereabouts are always itemized); the foregrounding of artworks about which we have more contextual data over objects about which we have less (or none); and an increased attention to the modern reception history of those canonical, archaeologically undocumented objects— such as those noted above or the Capitoline Brutus (bequeathed by a cardinal to the City of Rome in 1564), the Munich Marius and Sulla (purchased by King Ludwig I of Bavaria in the early nineteenth century) and many others. It is a call, in other words, for greater epistemological and methodological consciousness in the practice of the writing and teaching of Roman art history. My arguments begin from the fact that the quality of our evidence for the dates, places of manufacture, use or reuse, and social significances of individual works of Roman art (particularly free-standing sculpture, which has attracted the lion's share of scholarly attention for over a century) varies widely. Some objects are found during methodical archaeological excavations of a particular ancient city, villa, temple, or tomb, which yield not only the object itself but the inscribed base upon which it was origi-nally erected, other surrounding works, and additional indications of ancient function or reception. Others may have been recovered during the digging of a well or the laying of a new road, in which case little, if anything, will have been revealed about the original site. Ancient artworks also sometimes ended up built into medieval walls or chucked into rivers; those findspots tells us nothing about original use. Furthermore, records of findspots, especially those from previous generations and centuries, are often rather vague (e.g. "from Athens").

A second premise, however, is my belief that as long as it is trust-worthy (e.g. not reported second-hand by a vendor), any information about an ancient artwork's final deposition has epistemological value. We do not know the original setting of the statue of Augustus found in 1910 beneath a house on via Labicana in Rome, nor that of the bronze head of a young man found in 1847 in a ravine outside a small village near Chieti and now in the Bibliothèque Nationale, nor those of the hoarded group of bronze statuettes discovered in 1964 by workers laying pipes in the Ambelokipoi neighborhood of Athens. And yet, in addition to ensuring these works' authenticity, the findspots *ground* our interpretations of them in some way. Its siting in Rome connects the veiled portrait with Augustus' ostentatious piety and respect for ancestral customs in the ancient capital. The bronze head from the Chieti countryside fits into a larger picture of Etruscan bronze-casting expertise. The discovery of the Ambelokipoi bronzes in a group offers insights into ancient practices of statuary replication and collecting.

Artworks lacking a recorded findspot, on the other hand, have no such grounding. We can never be certain that they are what they seem to be, regardless of when they surfaced, their fame, the number of decades or centuries they have spent in prestigious collections, or the renown of the scholars who have studied them. Formal analysis is an invaluable tool, requiring sensitivity and extensive training. Done well, it not only illuminates an artwork's noteworthy features but may also reveal much about the training of its maker, the priorities of its patron, and its use over time. But its power to securely pinpoint the date and place of an ancient object's manufacture is, in my view, often overestimated. In this book, I will refer to *the attribution of an object to a particular time and place based strictly on formal and stylistic analysis* as connoisseurship. As I will argue in Chapter 3, connoisseurship in Roman art history presumes a great deal of regional and chronological uniformity of style on the part of ancient artists and relatively little personal or particularized input on the part of patrons—as well as little ability to accurately replicate these styles on the part of modern artists (forgers). These are risky assumptions— shaky ground upon which to build complex, specific narratives about ancient practices, beliefs or values. While the information yielded by archaeological context is often imprecise and always inflected by subjective interpretation, a documented findspot at least tethers the work to some piece of objective fact external to the work itself (cf. Neer 2005). A sculpture found in a secondary context at Ephesus must be dated on stylistic evidence, but its antiquity, and its association with Ephesus during the city's *floruit*, are secure facts. No amount of formal analysis, no matter how skilled, of an object that first surfaced on the art market can offer as firm a foundation for subsequent historical interpretation.

I will use the terms "grounded" and "ungrounded" to describe Roman artworks with and without (respectively) a known findspot. I offer this coinage because existing vocabulary, in my view, misses the mark. The most common pair of terms, "provenanced" and "unprovenanced," has in fact exacerbated the problem by blurring a critical distinction. Derived from the French *provenir* ("to come from"), "provenance" refers, by etymology and convention, to both findspot and ownership history (and sometimes to other matters still, such as the place of manufacture or the source of the material; Joyce 2012). An artwork such as the Barberini Togatus—first recorded in a Barberini family inventory in 1627 as a gift from a member of the Colonna family—would never be described as "unprovenanced," even though we are ignorant of its findspot, and even though that lacuna impedes our interpretation of the work (see Chapter 3; on the Barberini documents, Lavin 1975, 78–79; Picozzi 2010). "Contextualized"/ "uncontextualized" is also problematic. To call a stray find such as the Bibliothèque Nationale head "contextualized" seems too generous. The term would be more meaningful if it were reserved for works about which we have more substantial data, such as the group of portraits from the imperial villa triclinium at Baia or those from the Sanctuary of Hercules Cubans in Trastevere. Furthermore, to brand the Barberini Togatus "uncontextualized" devalues its richly documented and histor- ically significant *modern* settings. We don't know where (or if) many of the canonical Roman sculptures came out of the ground, but we do know a great deal about their various contexts since then—in circu- lation on the market, in collections, in the reception of the classical past and the formation of taste, and in the development of academic art history and archaeology. As I will argue for the Fonseca bust in Chapter 1, these modern contexts deserve more scholarly attention. Also frequently used to contrast the differing origins of various ancient artworks are the terms "licit" and "illicit." As I will discuss in Chapter 5, however, this dichotomy describes a set of issues quite different from those considered in this book, issues related to the market, not to epistemology.

As with all of these pairs, "grounded / ungrounded" runs the risk of over-simplification and loss of nuance. Both categories in fact contain within them a long, sliding, epistemological scale. For example, at one extreme in the former category (i.e. very grounded) are the pair of statues of L. Antonius Claudius Dometeinos and his neice, Claudia Antonia Tatiana, found intact, together with their original, inscribed bases in what appears to be their original setting, flanking the entrance to the Bouleuterion at Aphrodisias. In this case, the secure, layered knowledge we have of these works in their ancient environment is a function not only of their preserved findspot, but of the fact that Aphrodisias is, as a whole, one of the most carefully excavated and responsibly published sites in the ancient world. The current display of these sculptures, together in one gallery in the on-site museum, further enhances their "groundedness," as they can easily be examined as a pair and in light of their actual ancient setting. At the other extreme (barely grounded) is the bronze head from Chieti and now in Paris, about which we have only a rough geographic indication of findspot.

Likewise, some ungrounded artworks present greater uncertainty about their ancient origins than others. The ability of formal analysis alone to compensate for missing archaeological data in the attribution of an object to a time and place in history depends to a certain extent on the type of object in question. For example: a particular type of portrait, sculpted on square limestone panels in high relief, depicting veiled, heavily jeweled women and/or togate men, with elongated eyes and relatively little physiognomic detail, was produced only at Palmyra, a caravan city in central Syria, only between the first and third centuries CE, and only for funerary purposes. Their abundance at the site has made these reliefs cheaper to loot than to forge. These facts, together with their distinctive style, mean that ungrounded specimens can be fairly securely attributed, through connoisseurship, to "Palmyra, first–third century" (and possibly even to a more specific date). By contrast, connoisseurial attributions are less reliable for those ungrounded works, such as veristic male portrait heads sculpted in marble, whose forms and styles were employed at many different times and places and for many different purposes throughout Roman history, and for which modern demand has long exceeded supply.

If our goal is to understand the functions and meanings of art in the Roman world, any secure findspot information is better than none, and more is better than less. This criterion should, in my view, play a greater role than it currently does in decisions about which objects are included in the scholarship on and teaching of Roman art.

Resonance and wonder

Formal analysis has a crucial role to play in the interpretation of any object—whether grounded or ungrounded—whose forms bear expressive content. But there is a long-standing tradition in many humanistic disciplines to dichotomize form and context. An eloquent formulation of this view appeared in a 1991 essay by Stephen Greenblatt, who argued that objects can exert two types of power over viewers, powers he calls "resonance" and "wonder":

> By resonance I mean the power of the displayed object to reach out beyond its formal boundaries to a larger world, to evoke in the viewer the complex, dynamic cultural forces from which it has emerged and for which it may be taken by a viewer to stand. By wonder I mean the power of the displayed object to stop the viewer in his or her tracks, to convey an arresting sense of uniqueness, to evoke an exalted attention. (Greenblatt 1991, 42)

The two powers are, in his view, mutually exclusive, insofar as objects of wonder demand "intense, indeed enchanted, looking," in which "the act of attention draws a circle around itself from which everything but the object is excluded, when intensity of regard blocks out all circumambient images, stills all murmuring [historical] voices." The more arresting the object, in other words, the less its context matters (similarly: Godau 1989).

The philosophical origins of Greenblatt's notion of "wonder" go back at least to 1790, when Immanuel Kant argued in the *Critique of Judgment* that beauty is, by definition, purposeless, and that the consideration of function can only hinder aesthetic judgment. The Kantian perspective evolved into a deeply entrenched formalist tradition in art history (Podro 1982, 9–11). Scholars such as Heinrich Wölfflin, Alois Riegl, Henri Foçillon, Ernst Gombrich, Clement Greenberg, James Ackerman, and Ivan Gaskell have all argued, with varying emphases, that what makes art art is its ability to transcend its original function and speak through pure form to viewers across time and place (e.g. Wölfflin 1899; Riegl 1901; Foçillon 1934; Gombrich 1950; Greenberg 1961; Ackerman 1963; Gaskell 1996).

This belief buttresses one side of the looting and repatriation debate currently roiling the art world. Collectors, some museum officials, and their allies argue that visually interesting artworks belong on display rather than hidden in the ground, even if their original context is unknown; and even if their acquisition ensures—by encouraging more looting—that the contexts of additional artworks will be lost in the future (e.g. Griffin 1989; Cuno 2004 and 2008; White 2005; Boardman 2006; Kennedy and Eakin 2006; de Montebello 2009; Watt 2009).

Those who value context more highly have naturally opposed this position. The most vocal group to do so are archaeologists, by which I mean those who excavate, and who, by training, often extract as much information from an object's physical environment as they do from the object itself. The debate over looted antiquities has had the unfortunate consequence of exacerbating an ostensible divide between art historians and archaeologists (note here that I am using these terms in their American sense; in many other countries, including England, Germany, and Italy, "archaeology" does not necessarily mean excavation, but in fact encompasses what Americans would call ancient art history as well). In the recent words of one archaeologist, "collectors and dealers prize ancient objects primarily as works of art and beauty, while archaeologists value them as artifacts embedded in archaeological contexts capable of yielding meaningful information about the ancient culture and society that produced them" (Elia 2009a, 241; similar views expressed by Coggins 1969; Wiseman 1984; Pedley 1997; Whitley 1997; Shanks 1996; Chippindale and Gill 2000; Gill et al. 2001; Brodie et al. 2002 and 2006). Many archaeologists follow the thinking of Paul Kristeller, who suggested that "art" as we know it wasn't invented until the eighteenth century (Kristeller 1951 and 1952; Platt and Squire 2010). According to this view, notions of pure, historically transcendant form slide perilously close to deeply suspect ones of ahistorical, universal beauty. Ancient objects should instead be understood as manifestations of "visual culture" or "material culture"—the understanding of which depends heavily on context (Ridgway 1986, with response by Hood 1986; Goldhill and Osborne 1994; Borbein, Hölscher and Zanker 2000, 15–16; Whitley 2001; Lundén 2004; Scott 2006). In this and in much of the recent literature, the binaries are conspicuous: archaeology vs. art history, academia vs. museums, context vs. form, artifact vs. art, history vs. beauty, resonance vs. wonder.

My basic argument—that the richness of an ancient artwork's findspot data should play a greater role in determining its prominence in our teaching, scholarship, and exhibitions—aligns me to a certain extent with these archaeologists. I share their outrage at the destruction of ancient sites caused by plundering, and do not doubt their claim that such looting occurs to supply the demand of collectors. I accept the Foucauldian premise that categories such as "art" do not exist "anterior to discourse," and that practitioners of formal analysis must guard against anachronistic value judgment. I disagree, however, with the notion that the analysis of form (or style) somehow precludes that of context, or that it cannot complement and enhance our understanding of ancient material culture. The Romans did, after all, expend considerable resources to create material objects that looked a particular way. Their appreciation of form is evident in, for example, the extreme refinements in their marble carving techniques. The artist of any given work made a multitude of formal choices that allowed the object to communicate the particular messages desired by the patron, messages of a social, political, familial, religious, or eschatological nature. The art historian, with his or her special training in the analysis of form, is well-equipped to discern and describe those choices as choices, and to interpret them in light of the patrons' larger concerns. Innumerable studies in the corpus of art historical literature have demonstrated that beauty does not preclude history; wonder does not preclude resonance.

The tension, as I see it, lies in the fact that ancient artworks generated meaning not through their forms alone, but also through those forms' interactions with their larger setting. Inscriptions, other works belonging to the same dedication, older works already on the site, the enframing architecture or monument, the location in the house, city, tomb, or temple—these were also carefully considered by the artist and patron, and could shape a particular work's meaning as strongly as its own forms did. Historians of Roman art, myself included, are aware of this; and yet I, like many, have continued to perpetuate the long-established canon of mostly ungrounded objects in my teaching. I also largely ignored the epistemological risks of relying on ungrounded comparanda in my scholarship (e.g. Marlowe 2006, 227, fig. 8). In this regard, the archaeologists' accusation that art historians devalue context is not entirely without merit.

Many scholars of Roman art have resisted these disciplinary habits. Their work, some examples of which will be discussed in this book, rejects the ostensible binaries, combining close observations of formal qualities with specific information about—and interpretation of— larger physical context in order to illuminate the social functions and meanings of particular works of Roman art. Such work is, in my view, more epistemologically sound than that focused on ungrounded objects whose historical tethering relies entirely on connoisseurship. It can also draw more specific and thus more historically illuminating conclusions.

I am pleased to be able to present these ideas in the context of the "Debates in Archaeology" series. They are offered neither as a manifesto nor as a rebuke to my colleagues but rather as a call for a critical conversation about methodology, epistemology, and the canon. As a teacher at a small liberal arts college, I am concerned in particular with how Roman art is presented to those who are encountering it for the first time, a concern that extends not only to what is happening in the classroom and in textbooks, but in museum galleries as well. It is also my hope that these observations about scholarly and museological practices might contribute a fresh perspective to the debate over ungrounded antiquities, whose focus on ownership has, in my view, eclipsed matters of epistemology.

1

Histories Modern and Ancient

A glimpse of the eighteenth century

To step into the Palazzo Nuovo wing of the Museo Capitolino in Rome is to step back in time. The final element of Michelangelo's design for the Piazza del Campidoglio to be completed, the "new palace" limns the piazza's northeastern flank, bounding it from the medieval complex of the Church of Santa Maria in Aracoeli just beyond. Since 1733, when Pope Clement XII purchased the 421 sculptures of the Albani holdings, added them to the few dozen already held by the Conservatori, and decreed that the ensemble be accessible to the public, the Capitoline Museum complex has housed one of the world's most important collections of ancient Roman art. The contents, installation, and decor of the Palazzo Nuovo galleries resulted from a brief but intense flurry of curatorial activity that took place between 1733 and 1769, when Pope Clement XIV began directing new acquisitions of ancient sculpture to the reorganized Vatican Museums. Since then, various changes have been made to other parts of the Capitoline Museum, including, across the piazza in the Palazzo dei Conservatori, the 2005 opening of a spectacular glassed-in exedra to showcase the bronze statue of Marcus Aurelius. But the sculpture galleries of the Palazzo Nuovo have scarcely been touched. As a result, rooms like the Sala degli Imperatori and the Sala dei Filosofi, with their heavy chandeliers, ornate stucco moldings, and crowded, double rows of heavily restored portrait busts displayed on continuous, open shelves, transport us back to the mid-eighteenth century (Fig. 1). These galleries are, effectively, period rooms, inviting us to behave not just as art-lovers but also as anthropologists, imagining what art-lovers did in a bygone era and culture.

Such musing is time well spent. The first art collection ever concep-
tualized from the outset as a public museum, the Museo Capitolino
profoundly affected the development not only of other European
museums, but also of Grand Tourism, classical scholarship, and
neoclassical taste (Paul 2007; Arata 1996 and 2008; Minor 2010,
190–215; Presicce 2010a and 2010b; Collins 2010; Paul 2012). Its first
director, the Marchese Alessandro Gregorio Capponi, consulted with
leading scholars, including Francesco Ficoroni and Cardinal Albani, to
carry out Clement XII's wish that the museum not only "promote the
magnificence and splendor of the papal state of Rome," but that it also
"further the education of young students in the liberal arts" (chirograph
of 1734; Arata 1994, 75). To this end, the Capitoline sculptures were
installed not in the fashion of the princely collections, where works
of varying subject matters, formats, media, and periods were inter-
mingled and displayed according to aesthetic criteria such as size and
color (Minor 2010, 203; Presicce 2010b, 21). Rather, like was displayed

Figure 1   Sala degli Imperatori, Capitoline Museum, Rome.

with like. In the Sala degli Imperatori, dozens of imperial portrait busts were (and still are) installed close together, at eye level, and in chronological order. The fluid sequence of great men (and their beautiful wives) presented a literal embodiment of Roman imperial history from the first to the fourth centuries CE. The display also encouraged close scrutiny and side-by-side comparisons. As one emperor gave way to another, one dynasty to the next, the attentive viewer could trace the evolution of sculptural style, from the restrained and highly classicizing modeling of Augustus' portraits, to the exuberant and expressive carving of the Flavian and Antonine coiffures, to the linear geometries of the late antique heads.

The Capitoline galleries thus facilitated the sort of positivist, empirical study of ancient remains that was advocated by eighteenth-century antiquarians such as the Comte de Caylus, Piranesi, and Winckelmann (Haskell 1993, 159–200; Pinelli 2010; Barbanera 2010; Minor 2010). Today, these essentially unchanged rooms present a time capsule of a different era's construction of the past and reveal some fascinating contradictions of Enlightenment thought. On the one hand, for example, they reflect the period's deep faith in empirical data. Equally apparent, however, is the willingness to tamper with that data to ensure that it shows what it is supposed to show. This is evident in the sculptures' heavy-handed restorations. The repristinations guaranteed that the ancient artworks would measure up to pre-existing ideals of classical perfection, which required, among other qualities, completeness and high finish. Thus exposed in the Sala degli Imperatori is a fundamental clash between scientific objectivity and moralizing imperatives, competing desires with which classicists would wrestle for the next two centuries (Turner 1981; Hingley 1990; Stray 1998).

The eighteenth-century history of some individual works in the Capitoline Museum is as rich as that of the galleries as a whole. The most famous portrait in the Sala degli Imperatori is the Fonseca bust, named after José Maria Ribeiro da Fonseca de Évora (1690–1752), the Franciscan friar who bequeathed it to the museum in 1740 (Fig. 2). It

Figure 2   Marble portrait of a young woman, known as the "Fonseca bust," Capitoline
Museum, inv. 434. Ficoroni states that it was discovered, together with other sculptures, in a
late antique wall at the Villa Casale (Rome) (Ficoroni 1744, 89); note, however, the absence
of any record of the bust in the Casale archives (Giordani 1989, 56), and the very fine state
of preservation. Gift of Father Fonseca of Évora to the Capitoline Museum in 1740.

depicts a young woman with a towering corona of ringlets, known as a "toupet," crowning her porcelain-smooth face. The polished surface is broken only by the long, thin band of incised eyebrows, which join over the bridge of her nose. Her cheekbones are subtly modeled, her lips plump but dainty. Her head is tilted wistfully to one side on a long swanlike neck. From the time it entered the museum, the figure was identified, on the basis of the hairstyle, as Julia, daughter of the Flavian emperor Titus, though it has recently been redated on stylistic grounds to the Trajanic or Hadrianic period (Fittschen and Zanker 1983, 53–4). The piece proved useful to two powerful men in their maneuvering through the uncertain waters of eighteenth-century papal politics. One was Marchese Capponi, who had been very close to Pope Clement XII. The purchase of the Albani collection, the foundation of the new museum, and his own appointment as director had all occurred at the Marchese's suggestion. Pope Clement had died in February 1740, however, and when, later that year, Father Fonseca's gift arrived at the Capitoline, Capponi thought carefully about how to use the donation to impress his new boss, Pope Benedict XIV. In his diary, the museum director reveals that he delayed installing the Fonseca bust in the Sala degli Imperatori for almost a month, until he could do so with dramatic flourish on the occasion of Benedict's first official visit to the museum:

> I waited until in his presence to add to the series the bust of Julia of Titus, the gift of Father Évora, substituting it for another, inferior bust of the same woman. No one else participated, neither the Senators [Conservatori] nor anyone else, and thus I alone, Alessandro Gregorio Capponi, president of said museum, performed these services. (Franceschini and Vernesi 2005, 106)

Capponi was clearly quite pleased with himself and this grandiose little gesture. But the man most honored by the piece was of course Fonseca. Born in Évora, Portugal, in 1690, the Father took his vows in 1714 at the Franciscan friary at the Church of Santa Maria in Aracoeli, adjoining the Capitoline hill in Rome and just a few dozen meters from

the Palazzo Nuovo (Fonseca's biography: di Apricena 2000, 225–65).
He quickly rose through the ranks. In 1727, Pope Benedict XIII named
him Procurator General of the Order, and in 1732, Minister General.
A member of numerous scholarly societies, Fonseca added a *lanificio*,
major library, and grand suite of apartments for himself to the Aracoeli
complex. He was also a formidable diplomat; under his leadership, the
Aracoeli became the base of the Portuguese royal presence in Rome.
He served King John V as Minister Plenipotentiary, single-handedly
reopening diplomatic relations between his native land and the Holy
See. But in 1739, for reasons that remain unclear but which may reflect
the shift of the Portuguese monarch's sympathies from the Franciscans
to the Jesuits, Fonseca began to fall out of favor. In May, 1740, he
was recalled to Portugal, quitting the Eternal City against his will on
October 1. He went on to serve as Bishop of Porto until his death in
1752, but there is no trace of him in the royal archives from this period.
Historian Marianna Brancia di Apricena sees in this silence Fonseca's
ostracism from the king's inner circles (di Apricena 2000, 227–9).

Fonseca's parting gift to the Capitoline Museum, the prestigious
institution next door to the Aracoeli whose rise to prominence
coincided with his own, arrived less than a month before his final
departure from Rome. As Director Capponi noted in his diary, Fonseca
meant for the bust to serve as a "souvenir of himself" (*una memoria
di sè*) (Franceschini and Vernesi 2005, 105). While a sensual portrait
of a young, elaborately coiffed Roman princess might seem an unlikely
proxy for a Franciscan friar, the sculpture clearly signals Fonseca's
erudition, refined taste, and comfort in the highest circles of power.
Capponi further notes that the pedestal was already inscribed with
a "record of the donation" when it entered the collection. Donor
inscriptions are relatively rare in the Capitoline Museum, and most
commemorate the generosity of Pope Benedict XIV rather than an
outside patron. (Of the 66 busts on view today in the Sala degli
Imperatori, for example, only three others are inscribed with the name
of the donor, and all three name Benedict XIV.) It thus seems likely that
the inscription was commissioned by Fonseca himself.

The text suggests an attempt on Fonseca's part to control how he would be remembered in the Eternal City after his departure. It reads:

EX DONO
R`MI P. JOSEPHI MARIAE
FONSECA AB EBORA
EX GEN'LIS ORD: MIN:
S. FRANCISCI
AC REG: LUSITAN: APUD S. S. MIN'RI

This can be translated as: "Gift of / the Reverend Father Jose Maria / Fonseca of Évora / Former General of the Order of Friars Minor / of St. Francis / and Royal Portuguese Minister to the Holy See" (transl. Joseph Connors). It is perhaps noteworthy that his office at the Aracoeli is grandly trumpeted over two lines, while his royal and papal services are squeezed onto one. Fonseca seems to downplay his identity as a diplomat (a role from which he had recently been disbarred), and emphasizes instead his position of absolute power in the learned society of Rome. The selectivity may, in fact, have been even more extreme, for there is some evidence to suggest that the original text made no mention of Fonseca's royal and papal duties at all. The sixth line's relative length, awkward position (squeezed onto the flange of the pedestal), and absence from an otherwise complete transcription of the text in a 1748 guidebook to the Capitoline Museum all suggest that it was a later addition (Bottari 1748, 83). At any rate, Fonseca's donation of this artwork to the Capitoline Museum ensured that his good deeds and benefactions outlived the memory of whatever misdeeds or misfortune had triggered his recall to Portugal.

More research is needed on the biographies of both Fonseca and the Fonseca bust; it would be interesting to know, for example, who (if anyone) added the last line of the inscription and why. But even without all the details, the episode offers a glimpse of the rich reception histories that remain to be written of the canonical ancient artworks in the Capitoline Museum. Studies such as that by Moritz Woelk on the reception of the Herculaneum Women in Dresden, Marina

Belozerskaya on the biography of the Tazza Farnese, Robin Brooks on the Portland Vase and Cristina Mazzoni on the She-Wolf all demonstrate the value of such work, not only for the fascinating stories they tell, but also for their exposure of the ways in which various modern filters have colored our understanding of the pieces (Woelk 2007; Belozerskaya 2012; Brooks 2005; Mazzoni 2010).

An uncertain view of the ancient world

The Fonseca bust is ubiquitous in scholarly literature, but in the literature on the ancient world, not the eighteenth century. It is, in fact, one of the most frequently reproduced works in Roman art history. A popular choice for the covers and frontispieces of general surveys and more specialized studies of Roman portraiture, women, hairstyles, and luxury, it features in the pages of many more (a few recent covers and frontispieces include Gourevitch and Raepsaet-Charlier 2003; Winter 2003; Fontanella 2009; Ramage and Ramage 2009; La Rocca et al. 2011; Andreae 2012). Much of the historiography concerns the date of its manufacture and the identity of the sitter, hypothesized through connoisseurship. The elaborate hairstyle, with forward-swept curls in the front, and long, thin braids pulled into a large bun in the back, matches those on coins depicting women of the late first-century CE Flavian imperial household (Buccino 2011, 370–2, with earlier bibliography). As we saw above, Capponi, for example, believed it represented Julia, the daughter of Emperor Titus. Recently, however, Klaus Fittschen and Paul Zanker have argued that the work's technical brilliance (evident particularly in the sculptor's skilled handling of the drill), its theatrical contrasts between light and shadow, and between smooth and rough surfaces, are more typical of works of a generation later, from the early second century CE (Fittschen and Zanker 1983, 53–4). As a result, other names have been proposed, such as Vibia Matidia, the niece of the Emperor Trajan (Kleiner 1992, 179; already in Hausmann 1959) or Domitia Longina, the long-surviving widow of Domitian (Andreae 2012, 36). Fittschen and Zanker's redating has significant implications. As Elizabeth Bartman has noted: "[T]hat a woman possessing the beauty and, presumably, wealth of the Fonseca sitter would be represented wearing a hairstyle some 30 years old strikes a major blow against the view that stylish women transformed their hairdos every few years" (Bartman 2001, 19). As we will see in Chapter 3, many attributions of date in Roman art historiography do indeed depend on tightly calibrated hairstyle chronologies. The new dating of the Fonseca bust may encourage a rethinking of these metrics (Wood 1999; Alexandridis 2004).

Beyond the question of its date and identification, the Fonseca bust appears frequently in scholarly discussions of women in the Roman world. With its high degree of finish, exceptionally intricate coiffure and coy demeanor, the piece seems the very embodiment of the views expressed by the ancient authors Martial and Juvenal about the vanity and frivolity of aristocratic women (discussed by Bartman 2001, 8; Mannsperger 1998; Stephens 2008, 125). So much is evident from the titles of some of the exhibitions in which the bust has featured: "Beauty and Luxury: Images and Documents of Life's Pleasures," held at the Castel Sant'Angelo in 1992 (Cappelli 1992, 61 and 80), "The Bath and the Mirror: the Care of the Body and Cosmetics from Antiquity to the Renaissance," held at the Musée de Cluny in 2009 (Bardiès-Fronty et al. 2009, 16 and 149), and "Luxury: the Pleasures of Life in Imperial Rome," held at the Museo di Antichità in Torino in 2009, where the bust starred in the section entitled "Beauty and vanity in imperial Rome" (Fontanella 2009, 254–77).

The Fonseca bust is thus deeply enmeshed in the historiography of Roman art. Our heavy reliance upon it is, however, inversely proportional to how much we actually know about its ancient history—far less than we know about its eighteenth-century history. In his 1744 guidebook to Rome's antiquities, Francesco de Ficoroni asserts that the work was found, along with a number of other sculptures, reused in a late antique wall recently excavated at the Villa Casale, near the church of S. Stefano Rotondo (Ficoroni 1744, 89). Although a secondary context, this findspot, if reliable, would not only affirm the bust's authenticity, but might also offer a hint about its original ancient setting, as this region of Rome was renowned for its sumptuous, aristocratic residences. The catalogs of two recent exhibits at the Capitoline Museum that included the bust ("Portraits: the Many Faces of Power" and "The Age of Equilibrium: Trajan, Hadrian, Antoninus Pius, Marcus Aurelius") repeat Ficoroni's assertion as fact (La Rocca et al. 2011, 394; La Rocca et al. 2012, 265). The claim needs further investigation, however. A late antique wall comprising many spolia was indeed discovered on the Casale property around 1730, but it is not clear why Ficoroni associated the bust with those finds. According to Capponi's diary, Fonseca claimed only to have purchased the bust from the Casale household, whose estate abutted his own. The extensive Casale collections came from diverse sources, both archaeological and commercial. Noting the absence of any reference to the bust in the family archives, Rita Santolini Giordani has expressed doubt that the Casali found the portrait during their excavations, or indeed that they ever even owned it (Giordani 1989, 56; contra Venetucci 1998, 40n. 23, who sees no reason to challenge Ficoroni's assertion). Furthermore, the condition of the bust, with, for example, its delicate yet mostly unbroken ringlets, seems inconsistent with a history of reuse as construction material.

The other piece of evidence external to the bust itself that could provide a clue to its ancient significance is an alabaster replica in the Archaeological Museum in Fiesole (Fig. 3). The fact of ancient replication, while not the same as archaeological "grounding" as I have defined it, would increase the likelihood of both the authenticity of the Fonseca bust and the sitter's imperial identity—although it would be far stronger evidence if the replica were itself grounded, which is not the case here. At any rate, in a 1959 article, Ugo Hausmann noted the close affinities between the two works, in particular the hairstyle, long slim neck, tilted angle of the head, and refined carving (Hausmann 1959). Hausmann also asserted the Capitoline version's priority based on its much more intricate carving of the ringlets and on the Fiesole replica's omission of the distinctive eyebrows. The evidence can, however, be

Figure 3 Alabaster portrait head of a young woman, replica of the Fonseca bust, Fiesole Archaeological Museum, inv. 2553. Findspot unknown. Purchased on the art market by Marchese Edoardo Albites and donated to the museum in the late nineteenth or early twentieth century.

read otherwise. Easily overlooked today on the shiny, white surface of the marble, the "monobrow" of the Fonseca bust would originally have called attention to itself nearly as forcefully as the toupet, for the incised hairs would almost certainly have been enhanced with paint. This unusual but not unique veristic detail must have been an identifying trait of the sitter (cf. the portrait identified as Matidia with a monobrow and very unusual hairstyle, found in 1874 near Termini; details and complete bibliography in La Rocca et al. 2011, 396–7). Its absence on the otherwise iconographically identical Fiesole head may indicate distaste for the monobrow on the part of a copyist with a different—possibly anachronistic—aesthetic sensibility. Also perhaps indicating the Fiesole head's modern manufacture is the fact, strangely unmentioned by Hausmann, that it is carved in alabaster, a stone rarely (if ever) employed for Roman imperial portraiture. A bust of Agrippina in the Museo Nazionale Romano has, for example, been widely condemned on the basis of its alabaster medium (Trillmich 1974, 196n. 63; di Leo 1989, 52–3; Anderson and Nista 1989, 51–3; de Nuccio and Ungaro 2002, 324). It is also worth noting that the Fiesole portrait was purchased by the gentleman collector Marchese Edoardo Albites on the art market in either the late nineteenth or early twentieth century. While not damning in and of itself, this fact, in light of the work's other anomalies, urges further caution. Neither Ficoroni's report of findspot nor the Fiesole head can thus serve as contextualizing evidence for the Fonseca bust.

The Fonseca portrait's ancient context might have shed light on its unusual iconography. The position and angle of the head in particular require explanation. The figure (whose neck is original, while the bust is a later, modern addition) appears to be gazing at something over her left shoulder, and reacts to what she sees by cocking her head to the side. What is the meaning of this gesture? That would have depended, of course, on the support into which the head was originally set, and its larger installation. In a tomb setting, the angle might have expressed a nostalgic or sentimental emotion. Looking out over a villa vista, she might have appeared wistful and contemplative, as if lost in thought. If a portrait of her husband were set up to her left, her gaze could have been read as loving and tender. Viewed in isolation today in the Capitoline Museum, however, the pose of the Fonseca head appears affected and coquettish, neither of which are qualities the Romans would have been likely to celebrate in a portrait of a high-status woman.

Other anomalies compound the misfortune of the Fonseca bust's lost context. Connoisseurship's basic *modus operandi* is to emphasize affinities between objects; thus does one build up and hone in on a plausible attribution (if x is like y, and y was made in fourth-century Britain, then x was made in fourth-century Britain). Because they cannot contribute to this process, unique features are often inadvertently downplayed. Scholars have thus always underscored the *conformity* of the Fonseca figure's coiffure to those of the Flavian women: a tall crown of short curls brushed forward in front, and long, thin braids coiled into a large bun in back. One can also argue, however, that this version of the hairstyle is unparalleled, insofar as no other grounded example of it sports long, corkscrew ringlets over the brow. Aside from the Fonseca bust and the head in Fiesole, I know of only one other (ungrounded) portrait that does so: a bust of a priestess at the Michael C. Carlos Museum in Atlanta, first documented in a catalog of the Canessa collection in 1915 (Jucker 1961, 70–1; Michael C. Carlos Museum 2011, 56) (the portrait of Marciana at the Boston Museum of Fine Arts also has long ringlets in front, but otherwise bears little resemblance to the Flavian styles; it is also ungrounded). Otherwise, the standard Flavian hairdo features small, flat pincurls (or "snail curls"), with hollow centers drilled straight into the mass of stone. A typical example, now in the Louvre, was found during Pietro Rosa's 1865–66 excavations just north of the Domus Tiberiana on the Palatine hill (Tomei 1999, 257–8 and 467; de Kersauson 1996, 38–9) (Fig. 4). A short drill-bit was used to create round, shadow-filled cavities about a centimeter deep. The stone was then cut away from around each curl to make them pop out individually. Sometimes, the cavities are set so close together that the effect is closer to a honeycomb than to individual curls. The conception, carving, and overall visual effect of the Fonseca figure's

Figure 4 Marble portrait head of a young woman with Flavian hairstyle, Louvre, inv. MA 1158. Discovered in the Domus Tiberiana on the Palatine hill in 1865 by Pietro Rosa, during excavations carried out on land recently acquired by Napoleon III; found together with a second female Flavian portrait, also in the Louvre (inv. MA 1193).

toupet differ dramatically from any of the grounded examples. The fully plastic, hanging coils are carved almost completely in the round. The sculptor also deployed a very long drill-bit to punch boldly straight up through the center of each lock, allowing light to circulate through and around the spiraling forms (see cover photo). Indeed, in the hands of this artist, light is a medium as much as stone. The term "chiaroscuro" is commonly applied both to this piece and to the sculpted Flavian hairstyle more broadly; but with its suggestion of a mere binary between dark and bright, it scarcely does justice to the complex tonal range and vividly three-dimensional effect of the Fonseca coiffure.

Although no grounded Roman portraits of which I am aware sport a tall crown of corkscrew curls over the brow, ringlets themselves do feature elsewhere. Grounded examples of long curling locks arrayed down the sides or backs of Roman heads include the portrait of Agrippina the Younger from the Tomb of the Licinii in the Ny Carlsberg Glyptotek (Fig. 5); the herm-portrait of Staia Quinta from the Sanctuary of Diana at Nemi (also in Copenhagen); the bust of a woman found together with two heads of Julio-Claudian princes in 1949 near the Forum of Nomentum; and a "Kassel-type" Apollo head found at a magnificent domus during demolitions for the via dell'Impero and now at Montemartini (Agrippina: Kragelund et al. 2003, 114, cat. no. 31; Staia Quinta: Fejfer 2008, 300–4; Nomentum: Anderson and Nista 1988, 47–51; Apollo: Bertoletti et al. 1997, 81). In all of these examples (and many others as well), the sculptor created the ringlets by drilling deep, parallel diagonal channels across the surface of long, narrow, solid cylinders of stone. As on the Nemi example, the locks sometimes terminate in a snail curl, whose center is a round, shadowed cavity punched straight into the surface. These forms bear little relation to the plastic, hollow-centered, dangling spirals that constitute the Fonseca portrait's front locks.

With these observations, I seek only to emphasize that the Fonseca bust's anomalies are substantial enough to warrant caution. Like all ungrounded antiquities, and especially such idiosyncratic pieces, it offers unreliable testimony to ancient practices. In introductory

Figure 5 Marble portrait head of a young woman, identified as Agrippina the Younger, Ny Carlsberg Glyptotek, inv. 751. Probably found in the Tomb of Licinii in 1884–5. Purchased by Count Tyszkiewicz and sold, along with 17 other portrait heads, to Carl Jacobsen via Wolfgang Helbig in 1887.

classrooms, such pieces run the risk of warping the next generation's understanding of the norms of Roman art; for even if the Fonseca bust is ancient (and we are unlikely ever to know for sure), the piece is hardly typical. Where the bust does deserve a place is in studies of eighteenth-century cultural history, the development of European museums, and the reception and historiography of classical art.

Clearer prospects

The inevitable limitations of the historiography on ungrounded objects are apparent when contrasted with the deep and wide-ranging historical interpretations possible for grounded works of free-standing sculpture and Roman art more generally. One of the best sources for these is the site of Aphrodisias in Caria, southwest Turkey. In its heyday a thriving provincial capital, Aphrodisias was located near a marble quarry, and Aphrodisian sculpture was exported across the Roman Empire. The city was abandoned in the seventh century CE, leaving behind a well-preserved urban ensemble, from which over 200 portrait statues alone have been recovered since the early twentieth century (Smith et al. 2006, 11). In 1905, French excavations in the area between the south agora and the Hadrianic baths uncovered several statues, four female and three male (one of which depicts a late antique emperor, possibly Valentinian), most of which are now in the Istanbul Museum. Two of them, of the same size, and sporting the same carving style and very similar iconography, appear to have been created as a pair (Fig. 6) (Smith et al. 2006, 58, 207–11, nos. 89 and 90 [entries by Sheila Dillon]). They sport typical Flavian, pincurl "toupet" hairstyles in front, which, along with the style of their carving, suggest a date in the late first or early second century. One figure wears a veil over the back of her head, and is portrayed in the guise of Ceres, wearing a heavy mantle and holding a pomegranate and ears of wheat in her left hand, following a well-established type. The other figure, whose hair is

Figure 6 Two female statues in marble, one wearing a peplos and one in the guise of Ceres, Istanbul Archaeological Museum, inv. 2268 and 2269. Found next to one another in 1905 at Aphrodisias by Paul Gaudin, in excavations at the northern part of the south agora's west stoa, which adjoins the palaestra court of the Hadrianic Baths. Also discovered here were two other female and three male statues (two of which are shown in Figure 7). Photo by permission of R. R. R. Smith.

gathered into a loose ponytail in the back, wears a peplos; she has lost both hands, and with them all her attributes.

These are not the most fully documented Aphrodisian statues. Their bases are missing, and the report of the 1905 discovery does not specify their exact positions. It is also possible that this was, at any rate, a secondary location, to which they were moved perhaps in late antiquity. Despite these losses of data, the figures, with their nearly complete bodies, specific urban environment, and, most importantly, each other, as well as the other statues they stood beside, suggest some of the complex, layered messages that the Romans used (and reused) portrait statuary to convey. Sheila Dillon sets their forms in dialogue not with other sculptures of similar typology from elsewhere in the empire, as art historians often do, but rather with each other, as ancient observers would have done (Dillon in Smith et al. 2006, 207–11; for the more traditional approach, e.g. on the Ceres type: Bieber 1977, 163–73; Davies 2008). Dillon treats the iconographic details like the elements of a semantic system that acquire meaning in relation to one another. Thus, the matching, striking toupets and similar physiognomy strongly unite the figures as a pair. At the same time, however, the veil, tighter arrangement of the hair, sagging chin, bags under the eyes, as well as the Ceres attributes mark one figure out as the elder of the two, and celebrate her matronly virtues, including her fertility. The peplos woman can, through the contrast, be understood most likely as the older woman's daughter, unmarried, young but full-grown, virtuous in her "conservative, old-fashioned modesty, even Athena-like virginity" (suggested by the peplos, a relatively unusual choice) (Dillon in Smith et al. 2006, 210). That the statues were relocated together to the stoa facing the Baths, or, at any rate, that they remained side by side for centuries after their initial dedication, suggests that their interdependence continued to be appreciated over time.

In an article on the Hadrianic baths at Aphrodisias, R. R. R. Smith returns to this pair, and to their discovery alongside statues made hundreds of years later, to emphasize the "ancient synchronic experience" of statuary (Smith 2007). The later neighbors of the

Figure 7   Two male statues in marble, both wearing the chlamys, known as the "Elder and Younger Magistrates," Istanbul Archaeological Museum, inv. 2255 and 2266. Found together with the female figures in Figure 6. Photo by permission of R. R. R. Smith.

mother–daughter pair included another duo, this time of fifth-century officials, both wearing the chlamys, which Smith has argued signaled not just a civic magistracy but a connection to the imperial center and to military authority (Istanbul Archaeological Museum, inv. 2266 and 2255; Smith 1999, 176–8) (Fig. 7). One of these chlamydati, sometimes identified as the elder of the pair, has a gaunt, bony face and thin lips, and wears a Trajanic style cap of short, flat locks of hair ("lank and unfashionable": Smith 2002b, 143). The other man, possibly younger, has a fuller, fleshy face, thick lips, and sports a bushy "wreath" hairstyle associated with Constantinople. He also wears an unusual, circular tonsure atop his head, which Smith interprets as a sign of his Christianity (but not of his membership of the clergy; the chlamys and hairstyle would seem to indicate an imperial office: Smith 2002b, 154–5). This pair, too, is strongly united by one distinctive feature (their cloaks this time, rather than their coiffure), and differentiated from one another through various other details, whose significance is enhanced in the comparison. Smith refrains from speculating, but one is left wondering if perhaps their 300-year-old female neighbors lent a certain nobility or legitimacy to the new officials; or if the installation did not in some way create two new couples, each office-holder paired with a venerable but age-appropriate companion, making a balanced and attractive foursome.

It is, of course, impossible to assess this without better records of the statues' exact positions at the time of their discovery. Nor does this picture account for the other two women (one a Pudicitia type and the other a Large Herculaneum Woman type) or the Theodosian emperor found here as well. What is clear is that the mother–daughter pair would, in one way or another, have been reactivated or reanimated by the installation of the portrait-statues of the new officials nearby. This observation offers a valuable corrective to a number of common art historical tendencies. These include our usual, narrow focus on the moment of a work's creation ("a useful form of historical investigation, but false to ancient reality, to ancient experience"; Smith 2007, 204) and our long-standing view of late antiquity as a time of cultural impoverishment. As Smith notes, although only about one-tenth the number of new statues seems to have been created in Aphrodisias between the fourth and seventh centuries, as compared to the quantity created between the first and fourth centuries, nevertheless, "quantity remains," so the "actual numbers on display increased during late antiquity" (Smith 2007, 204); furthermore, that quantity lent itself to creative and possibly ideologically laden appropriations and reconfigurations. "Ancient statues rarely stood in solitary splendour as in modern city squares; they were displayed in concentrated organic groups that shifted and grew and gave new shades of meaning, association and reference to those present" (Smith 2007, 204; note the affinities here with the archaeological and anthropological theory known as "object biographies": Kopytoff 1986; Gosden and Marshall 1999; Schiffer and Miller 1999).

Had, say, the mother-figure from Aphrodisias surfaced on the art market, none of these nuances about her rich, shifting ancient meanings would have been perceptible. It would have been identified as a private portrait from around 100 CE of a woman in the guise of Ceres, wearing a Flavian-style toupet, and compared to replicas in the Louvre, the Vatican, and at Ostia (as it is in Bieber 1977, pl. 124). Like Smith's and Dillon's, the best scholarship on Roman art privileges works about which we have multiple data points and combines sensitive readings of artists' formal choices with evidence external to the objects themselves. For public statuary, the latter might include dedicatory inscriptions; inclusions in and exclusions from larger statue groups; relative positioning or formal echoes within that group; the civic architectural benefaction in which the work stood; other images of the same figure from different locations in a given city; and many other aspects (e.g. Price 1984; Bol 1984; Boatwright 1993; Dillon 1996; Rose 1997; Pappalardo 1997 and 2005; Smith 1998; Boschung 2002; Mayer 2010; Longfellow 2011; many other examples could be named). By attending to sculpture in its larger physical context, the field has been able to move away from a relatively simple model of top-down propaganda toward subtler ones such as gift-exchange and self-fashioning. We are learning more and more about the ways in which public monuments and images served to negotiate between client and patron, subject and emperor, one city and another, expressing status relations, political allegiances, and cultural identity.

In the funerary realm, the preservation of sculptural ensembles has allowed for similarly expansive readings. At the Mausoleum of Claudia Semne, Claudia was portrayed five times and her son, Marcus Ulpius Cotronensis, four (Wrede 1971; Bignamini and Claridge 1998; Koortbojian 2007 and Cadario 2011, 217–21, give other examples of multiple images of the same figure from single contexts). Claudia's multiple portraits add up to a complex picture of the ideal wife and mother: she is beautiful and fertile (in the guise of Venus), she brings a prosperity to the household through her dowry and good management (Fortuna), and offers hope for the future of the family line (Spes). Her son, meanwhile, is portrayed as a well-educated citizen (in two togate statues, each with a scroll-box at its feet), as well as a brave, manly hunter (in a nude statue in the guise of Meleager or Adonis). Together his images constitute the complete package: a man of words and of action, in command in both the urban and natural environments, a sound mind in a healthy body. Again, none of these layered, integrated readings would have been possible had these portraits surfaced individually on the market. In the private realm, Michael Squire has recently contributed to our understanding of the ancient reception of the Sperlonga sculptures by reading them together with a ten-line ekphrastic epigram praising their evocative power, which was inscribed on a plaque and installed in the cave in late antiquity (Squire 2009, 202–38). Likewise in the domestic realm, John Clarke, Bettina Bergmann, and Rebecca Molholt have demonstrated the necessity of reading paintings and mosaics in light of what else was in the visual field of the observer (Clarke 1991; Bergmann 1994 and 2002; Molholt 2011; also Bartman 1988 and 1991; Warden and Romano 1994).

As all of this excellent scholarship makes clear, the messages communicated by works of Roman art were strongly shaped by multiple elements in their ancient environment. There are many indicators, however, that the larger field of Roman art history—as evident in its common denominators of undergraduate survey textbooks and museum installations, as well as in much of the scholarship not explicitly focused on works from a particular site—has yet to fully absorb the implications of these findings. The next chapter will examine some of the ways in which older models of art historical analysis, with their privileging of ungrounded works and/or other signs of indifference to context, continue to prevail.

2

Indifference to Context

Chicken and egg

The discipline of Roman art history developed in the nineteenth and early twentieth centuries chiefly around the standing monuments in the city of Rome such as the Column of Trajan and the Arches of Titus and Constantine. Questions of style predominated at first (Wickhoff 1895; Riegl 1901; Strong 1907; Rodenwaldt 1935). Soon, however, the European experiences of dictatorships and total war drew attention to the ideological content of these state-sponsored images of emperors, their conquests, and their triumphs (e.g. Alföldi 1935; L'Orange and von Gerkan 1939; Hamberg 1945). Historical and political analysis was possible because these monuments could be interpreted in conjunction with a number of externally grounding data points. These include the other images positioned around each individual relief, the monument's dedicatory inscription(s), and/or its particular location in the ancient capital. The messages that can be read into the work as a whole—the relationship between military victory and political legitimacy, the divine sanction of Roman military expansion, the benefits of conquest by Rome, the ruler's relationship to his predecessors, and so on—are thus larger and more nuanced than what, say, any one relief's own forms could have communicated. The whole is more than the sum of its parts.

At the same time, another strand of Roman art historiography developed from the early catalogs of the major collections, including that of Walther Amelung on the Vatican, Henry Stuart Jones on the Capitoline Museum, Wilhelm Furtwängler on the Munich Glyptothek, and Carl Blümel on the collections in Berlin, as well as Wolfgang

Helbig's earlier guide to all the antiquities in the public collections in Rome (Helbig 1891; Amelung 1903–08; Furtwängler 1907; Stuart Jones 1912; Blümel 1933). J. J. Bernoulli and Richard Delbrueck pioneered the study of Roman portraiture using much of the same material (Bernoulli 1882–94; Delbrueck 1912 and 1914). By the time Werner Technau and Herbert Koch published their respective Roman art surveys in the 1940s, a canon of sorts had been established (Technau 1940; Koch 1949). In addition to standing works of architecture, the figural monuments in Rome, and the wall-paintings from the Vesuvian region, the other major category of material in these handbooks consisted of the best preserved (and/or heavily restored), mostly ungrounded free-standing sculptures in the major museums in Rome and other European capitals and cities. These included many that still feature prominently in our handbooks today, such as the Fonseca bust, the laurel-crowned Bevilacqua Augustus in Munich (which surfaced in the collection of Count Bevilacqua in Verona in 1589), and the Capitoline Brutus (recorded by Aldovrandi in the collection of Cardinal Rodolfo Pio da Carpi in 1556).

That most of these objects should have lost their associated contextual data is hardly surprising. For much of the period during which ancient art has been collected, specific historical or physical context played almost no role in its appreciation, and was thus rarely thought worth preserving. The laws and economics of the art market have also contributed to the erasure of findspot information. To identify the exact site where a valuable ancient artwork was discovered is to create a host of potential claimants (landowners, developers, government, papal, or museum authorities, etc.) who might block the sale, demand a cut of the proceeds or make arrests (Tyszkiewicz 1898; Kragelund et al. 2003; Dyson 2006; Cagiano de Azevedo 2008). Furthermore, the sooner the findspot is forgotten, the fewer the accomplices to theft or illegal exportation, and the more legitimate the claims that all parties have acted in "good faith" (Watson and Todeschini 2006; Silver 2009; Felch and Frammolino 2011).

Unlike the historiography on the standing monuments in the

ancient capital (or the more recent literature, discussed at the end of the previous chapter, on works from other particular sites), studies of the beautiful, ungrounded sculptures in the prestigious museums necessarily addressed—and continue to address—questions for which knowledge of the work's ancient, physical context is unnecessary. To stay with the Fonseca bust, consider this encapsulation of the current state of scholarship, which typifies the approach to ungrounded objects:

> Portrait sculpture of the Flavian period dealt with new problems. Perhaps the most challenging was the elegant style of female hairdos that became popular at this time. Typical was a mass of curls piled high on the head and standing up in ringlets over the bare forehead. The style was undoubtedly initiated by one of the imperial wives, but it must have caught on quickly among the fashionable women of the day. The most beautiful example is the head of a lady [the Fonseca bust], now thought to have been carved some years later but in the Flavian style. Her long elegant neck curves gracefully upward as it supports the strong-chinned, heavy-browed, yet delicate face. The curls of her magnificent coiffure are drilled with deep holes in the center, providing a fine example of chiaroscuro – where the contrast of light and shade is used for artistic effect. Individual hairs are chiseled out on the surfaces, while defiant wisps of short hairs, escaping the ordered pattern, lie gently on the back of the lady's neck. (Ramage and Ramage 2009, 184)

The "new problems" on which this textbook focuses are those of the sculptor. It could scarcely have done otherwise. The (ostensibly) ancient work of art with no ancient grounding exists as an indexical trace only of what some past artist once did. The problems, motivations, and actions of the patron, at a prior moment, or of ancient audiences, at later moments—these are lost to us. And so the object is held up before us, and we are invited—and taught—to imagine the sculptor alone in his studio, faced with the challenge of depicting the frothy confection of the latest hairstyle, to behold and to admire the details of his stunning solution. Nothing in this passage draws

attention to the gaps in our knowledge about this work's ancient history
or indicates that there might be any other way of thinking about it
beyond the actions of the artist who produced it. Indeed, the literature
on ungrounded objects makes purely formal approaches like this seem
inevitable, historically uncontingent, natural, and self-sufficient. And
this, in turn, makes matters such as context seem dispensable.

Which came first, the prioritization of purely stylistic questions,
such as those considered in the passage cited above, or the canonical
status of ungrounded objects like the Fonseca bust? The corpus of
Roman art has expanded vastly since the formation of the collections
in Rome, Paris, Copenhagen, Berlin, Munich, London, New York, and
Boston (on which see Marchand 1996; Giuliani 2000; Dyson 2006,
133–71). Major sculptural finds have emerged in excavations at Alba
Fucens, Amelia, Aphrodisias, Aquileia, Astigi (Ecija, Spain), Baia,
Butrint, Caesarea, Carthage, Cartoceto, Cyrene, El Ruedo (Cordoba),
Ephesos, Formia, Gerasa, Izmir, Marseille, Narona (Croatia), Nemi,
Perge, Sardis, Sessa Aurunca, Sestino, Side, Stobi (Macedonia), and
many other sites. Some of the excavations have been well-published.
But if scholars choose to focus their research and teaching on questions
of stylistic evolution, or on the exceptional accomplishments of
individual artists such as the creator of the Fonseca bust, on portrait
identifications or hairstyle taxonomies, they may see little or no reason
(not even the epistemological ones) to "redo all our powerpoints" (as
one colleague put it to me) and replace the canonical, ungrounded
objects on which they were trained for relatively newly discovered,
better-contextualized ones.

The preference for beautiful objects over less beautiful ones also
plays a role in determining which do and which don't appear in
scholarly and popular literature. Take, for example, the contrasting
fates of two pairs of portraits of Septimius Severus and Julia
Domna, which surfaced within a few years of each other. One pair
consists of full statues of the imperial couple, discovered in 1968 at
the Hydreion at Perge, together with a statue of a local priestess-
benefactor, Aurelia Paulina, as well as a number of reliefs and lengthy

Figure 8 Marble portrait statues of Septimius Severus and Julia Domna, Antalya Archaeological Museum (Özgür 2008, nos. 38 and 39). Found in 1968 in front of the monumental nymphaeum at Perge, along with many other sculptures, reliefs, and inscriptions.

Figure 9 Marble busts of Septimius Severus and Julia Domna, Bloomington, Indiana University Art Museum, inv. 75.33.1 and 2. Findspot unknown. Said to have been purchased in Germany shortly after World War II. Gift of Thomas T. Solley.

inscriptions (Fig. 8). Announced in several preliminary reports, the Hydreion and its associated sculpture was fully published by the excavator Arif Mansel in 1975 in the *Istanbuler Mitteilungen* (Mansel 1975). The ensemble is now at the Antalya Museum. Also in 1975, Thomas Solley, Director of the Indiana University Art Museum, donated to his own institution a beautiful, immaculately preserved, ungrounded pair of busts depicting the same imperial couple (acquisition announced in the *Art Journal*, 1975-6, 153-4) (Fig. 9). Museum files note that the busts are said to have been acquired in Germany shortly after World War II, and that Jiri Frel, then curator of ancient art at the Getty, reported in a 1977 telephone call that they were discovered near the Terme Museum, during construction of the Metropolitana (subway).

Within three years of the busts' arrival in Bloomington, Klaus Fittschen had come to see them and published a full, richly illustrated assessment (Fittschen 1978). Since then, they have featured in at least four studies of Severan portraiture or imagery, an influential exhibit and symposium on women in the ancient world, a study of hairstyles and recarving, and a survey of Greek and Roman sculpture in America, as well as the two leading Roman art textbooks and another on Roman Britain (Vermeule 1981, 345, Figs. 297, 298 and color plate 28; Nodelman 1982, 116, Fig. 18; Baharal 1992, 114; Raeder 1992, 191 and pl. 67. 1-4; Kleiner and Matheson 1996, 81-84, Figs. 42 and 43; Kleiner and Matheson 2000, 5, Fig. int. 2 and cover photo; De la Bédoyère 2006, 61, Fig. 54; Galinsky 2008, 6, Fig. 8; Ramage and Ramage 2009, 285-7, Figs. 9.4 and 9.7; Kleiner 2010, 234-5, Figs. 16.6-7; Lusnia forthcoming). The Severan portraits from Perge have, by contrast, largely dropped off the radar. To my knowledge, they have appeared in three portraiture studies and nowhere else (Ghedini 1984, 135, Fig. 18; Mickocki 1995, 210n. 412; Alexandridis 2004, 199, Fig. 49.1), although the Perge Hydreion itself and some of its other sculptures have received more attention (Schmidt-Colinet 1991; Dorl-Klingenschmid 2001, 229-30 and 362; Fejfer 2008, 362-7; Longfellow 2011, 185-88).

The relative neglect of the richly contextualized Severan portrait-statues from Perge, and the attention lavished on the Severan busts in Bloomington, follows a pattern in Roman art historiography. Like the preference for the Fonseca bust over the Flavian woman from the Palatine hill or the mother–daughter pair from Aphrodisias, here, too, extraordinary, visually spectacular, ungrounded works are favored over their grounded counterparts, which are almost invariably less unusual and less beautiful. Beyond pure aesthetics, practical matters can also, of course, play a role. In the preface to the first edition of their textbook, Nancy and Andrew Ramage state explicitly that they have favored works in U.S. collections where possible, "so that American students will have a better chance of looking at some of the originals" (Ramage and Ramage 1991, 9). It is also less expensive for a small American museum to borrow domestically than from abroad (Kleiner and Matheson 1996). Crisp, clear images of the Indiana busts are, furthermore, easily accessible on Artstor, whereas there are no images on Artstor of the Perge pair, and the lighting in the Antalya Museum makes them difficult to photograph.

It often requires a concerted effort to acquaint oneself with archaeological finds, even major ones from decades past. It is increasingly common to house them in small, municipal museums close to the sites where they were discovered (Giuliani 2000, 83). This practice encourages both scholars and artlovers to understand the objects in close association with their ancient setting (as well as directing more of the tourist economy to local communities). It also means, however, that one does not come upon such objects serendipitously. A visit to a regional archaeological museum requires significantly more advanced planning and travel—and often the rental of a car—than a trip to the Louvre or the Vatican. Tenure clocks, budgets, or family obligations may prohibit researchers from undertaking far-ranging voyages. (It is surely no coincidence that some of the most complete genre and typology studies in the field, with the widest-ranging evidence, have been produced by German scholars granted the government-supported *Reisestipendium* of the German Archaeological Institute, which sends them on a full year of directed traveling, at an early stage in their careers, to archaeological sites across the Mediterranean.) Furthermore, small, regional museums are often at the mercy of larger political forces; accessibility may suffer from underfunding and erratic hours. The Fier Archaeological Museum in western Albania, which contains the impressive sculptural finds uncovered at nearby Apollonia over several decades before and after World War II by French and then Albanian archaeologists, was closed from 1991 until 2011. Such museums also often lack print or online catalogs of their collections, further impeding incorporation of their holdings into mainstream scholarship.

Historical, aesthetic, institutional, and practical factors have thus all contributed to the prominence of ungrounded artworks in much of the historiography on Roman art. Methodological indifference to context has also played a significant role, despite the large body of work noted at the end of Chapter 1, work that is deeply attentive to the dynamic interrelationships between artworks and their settings. The remainder of this chapter will discuss some of the discipline's context-indifferent or even context-negating practices.

Inconsistent labels

The "tombstone" portion of labels in museum galleries and catalogs, the photo captions in textbooks, scholarly monographs and articles, and the "slide ID" component of many undergraduate art history exams commonly identify featured works by artist's name (if known), title, date, medium, and current location. For ancient works, the checklist sometimes also includes findspot, but usually with less exacting standards. Often, findspot is mentioned only when it is relevant to the argument at hand. The unknown findspots of ungrounded works are rarely acknowledged; it is common to give ownership history instead. This sleight of hand, facilitated by the intrinsic ambiguity of the term "provenance," has been criticized by others (discussed in the Introduction; Coggins 1998, 57; Chippindale and Gill 2000, 467–8).

The problem goes further, however. From this basic semantic ambiguity, the range of accepted answers to the question "Where from" has expanded, with little critical attention paid to epistemology. In fact, in many publications on ancient art, as many as eight different types of information might appear interchangeably as "provenance": good findspot data ("from Acquarossa, monumental building F, where the slabs apparently adorned the internal portico"), vague findspot data ("from Cologne"), hypotheses seemingly based upon connoisseurship ("from Asia Minor"), hypotheses whose basis cannot be determined ("from Rome"), rumor ("said to have been found in Alexandria"), ownership history ("from the Farnese collection"), acknowledgment of no provenance ("findspot unknown"), and silence.

Each of these types of information (with the exception of the last) has its uses, but the laconic presentation compromises their value. The reliability of "said-to-be" statements, for example, often depends entirely on *who* said it, when, and what the speaker's interests were (avoiding the detection of a theft? dodging import restrictions? enhancing an object's prestige? preserving knowledge?) (some examples: Hartswick 2004; Spanel 2001, 91n. 17; Kragelund, Moltesen, and Østergaard 2003; see also the discussion in Chippindale and Gill 2000). Disciplinary convention, however, requires neither disclosure nor discussion of the speaker's identity. Colleagues tell me that they never trust said-to-be reports, and simply discount them. But that too may be an epistemologically unsound practice, leaving potentially valuable information on the table. With no data by which to assess it, however, there is little alternative.

Even more troubling, in my view, are the claims whose basis cannot be determined at all. What do labels like "from Rome," "from Greece," or "from Asia Minor" mean? Are these facts or hypotheses? If they are facts, how are they known? By a vague but reliable findspot report? What makes it reliable? If they are hypotheses, what are they based upon? What are the closest comparanda? Sometimes uncertainty is clearly indicated, for example "probably from Rome" or "possibly from Constantinople." Does that mean that the other labels in the same publication not so flagged are solid facts? And again, on what basis are those alleged origins deemed possible or probable? Without more information by which to assess the merits of the suggestions, readers must either take them on faith or ignore them.

More harmful than any one of these particular formulations, however, is their indiscriminate exchange for one another in catalog entries and photo captions that set aside a single data field for "provenance." This widespread practice blurs the fundamental distinction between fact and hypothesis, and suggests a lack of methodological awareness (Muscarella 2000, 14; Smith 2002a, 75). Firsthand reports of findspot, secondhand reports of findspot, straightforward acknowledgments of unknown findspot, ownership history, and suppositions based on style all contribute to our knowledge and understanding of the object, but they are not interchangeable. They belong to distinct discourses, answer different sets of questions, and carry different epistemological weight.

Grounded and ungrounded, side by side

Both of the leading textbooks marketed to American undergraduates pair the Bevilacqua Augustus with the via Labicana Augustus, presenting them as equally reliable testimony of the emperor's self-fashioning, without discussing the very different paths by which they reached us (Kleiner 2010, 67–8; Ramage and Ramage 2009, 124). Like the unsystematic labeling practices described above, such undifferentiated presentations of grounded and ungrounded objects further suggest—and pass on to the next generation—a disinterest in both context and epistemology.

This too can be found in the literature at all levels. The highly specialized volumes of the Herrscherbild series, sponsored by the German Archaeological Institute, give equal weight to grounded and

Figure 10 Marble portrait heads conventionally identified as "Marius" and "Sulla," Munich, Staatliche Antikensammlungen und Glyptothek, inv. GL 319 and GL 309. Findspot unknown. The Marius portrait has been identified with an engraving of a sculpted bust in the Barberini collection in the Tetius description of 1642. In 1814, Ludwig I of Bavaria purchased the bust from the dealer V. Cammuccini via his agent M. von Wagner. The Sulla portrait was in Palazzo Ruspoli, and was sold to Ludwig I between 1811 and 1812 by the dealer P. M. Vitali, who claimed that it had formerly belonged to the Crescenzi and Caetani collections. Photo by Egisto Sani.

ungrounded specimens in their identifications of imperial portrait types. The 2011 exhibition of Roman portraiture at the Capitoline Museum featured a particularly extreme juxtaposition of contrasting epistemological certainty. The so-called Marius and Sulla from Munich faced across the main gallery to two heads from Delos (La Rocca et al. 2011, 164–5 and 170–1, with previous bibliography). The former are two of the least secure works in the Roman art canon (Fig. 10). Their style, iconography, and scale suggest that they were created as a pair, but they surfaced in the hands of two different dealers, who offered different ownership histories, at different dates in the early nineteenth century (although Bernoulli identified the "Marius" with a bust formerly in the Barberini collection, which had already been illustrated by Hieronymus Tetius in 1642: Bernoulli 1882, vol. 1, 82n. 1;

Faedo and Frangenberg 2005, 475 and pl. XLVI). Both were eventually sold to King Ludwig I of Bavaria. Due to this convoluted history, and to their many departures from Roman portrait norms (e.g. their sharply twisting necks, curious bulbous formations at the juncture of the brow and nose, sharp eyebrow lines, enormous, bulging, deep-set eyes, and partially open mouths), there is no consensus regarding their date or function (late Republican? From the Tomb of the Scipii? Copies of Republican originals installed in the *summi viri* gallery of the Forum of Augustus? Hadrianic copies of Augustan copies of Republican originals? Nineteenth-century? See discussion and bibliography in La Rocca et al. 2011).

The Delos portraits, by contrast, are among the most richly contextualized works of Republican portraiture from anywhere in the ancient world. The Romans made the sacred island of Delos into a commercial freeport in 166 BCE. The island thrived as a center of the pan-Mediterranean slave trade until its sack in 88 BCE by a general of Mithridates VI. French excavations, ongoing since the late nineteenth century, have uncovered nearly two dozen portraits on the island (Marcadé 1996). One of the portraits in the Capitoline exhibit was found in 1905 in a private house, while the other was discovered that year in the "Agora des Italiens," a trapezoidal courtyard near the port, begun around 120 BCE and probably associated with the slave trade (Mastino 2008; Trümper 2008). The porticoes of the agora were embellished with 29 statue niches; excavators have discovered 14 associated statue bases, one body and two heads. The inscribed bases inform us that the statues were set up by Italian freedmen—former slaves grown rich on the enslavement of others—in honor of their senatorial patrons and financial backers (Rauh 1993, 198–200, 232). The Delos heads in the Capitoline exhibition lack the dramatic intensity of the Munich portraits, but their forms are striking nonetheless, with their polished surfaces, skillful treatment of subcutaneous bone and muscle, cropped hair, deep-set eyes, and, in one case, expressive turn of the neck. They feature prominently in debates about the origins of veristic portraiture, thanks to their precise chronology and their stylistic affinities both with idealizing images of Hellenistic rulers and with the veristic portraits associated with Republican senators (Rose 2008, with previous bibliography).

The layered, rippling historical significance of the Delos portraits, engendered not just by their forms but also by their physical setting and associated finds, contrasts with any possible reading of the Munich heads, whose inward-facing, purely formal, and entirely speculative quality is unavoidable due to the portraits' lack of archaeological grounding. But the Capitoline exhibit did not comment explicitly on this inequality. The catalog is exemplary—and highly unusual—in its painstaking discussion of each work's origins and ownership history, and in its thorough summary of the historiography (including the doubts about the Munich heads' authenticity). But by not prioritizing grounded works over ungrounded ones in any way, the show implicitly suggested that context is but one among many data points in the analysis of ancient works of art, no more or less important than any other.

Grounded but now uncontextualized

Even in cases of artworks with richly documented findspots, ancient context is not always foregrounded. It often seems that the more famous and/or visually interesting the object, the less its ancient context is discussed. The spectacular bust of Commodus in the guise of Hercules was found alongside a pair of tritons in an underground chamber of the imperially owned Horti Lamiani in Rome in 1874. Though they are all displayed together in the Conservatori wing of the Capitoline Museum, together with other sculptures recovered at the site, the tritons are rarely included in discussions or photographs of the famous bust (which tend to focus either on the masterful carving or the emperor's megalomania). Similarly, in his influential 1986 study of Republican portraiture, Luca Giuliani analyzed the famous image of Pompey in Copenhagen not as an object of the first century CE (which its archaeological context indicates it is) but rather as a transparent stand-in for the lost original portrait of Pompey from a century earlier (Giuliani 1986, 67–72). Giuliani read the fundamental "ambiguity" of the image, with its combination of Hellenistic pathos and Republican verism, as a reflection of clashing mid-first-century BCE concerns about the military basis of political legitimacy, the *mos maiorum*, and Rome's relationship to Greece. But he had little to say about the tomb in which this actual portrait was found, or about the 15 other portraits of members of the Licinii Crassi clan, ranging in date over the first two centuries CE, with which it was displayed (Giuliani 1986, 58; for a more contextual perspective, see Kragelund 2002; on the discovery: Kragelund, Moltesen, and Østergaard 2003 as well as van Keuren 2003, who doubts that all 15 portraits came from the tomb).

A comparable disinterest in an object's ancient display context can occur in museums as well, and not just in the northern European and American museums where ungrounded antiquities predominate over grounded ones. With one important exception (the material from the Theater at Perge; see Chapter 5), the Antalya Museum, for example, systematically breaks up excavated sculptural ensembles, redistributing their components according to the museum's own taxonomies and design principles. In 1970 and 1971, excavators at Perge's north nymphaeum recovered statues of Hadrian and his family members, as well as those of Zeus, Artemis, and Apollo. The ensemble, in antiquity, would have advertised the advantageous interrelationships among the supreme god, the supreme earthly ruler, and the gods most sacred to Perge (where there was a major cult to Artemis; Apollo is her brother). This highly meaningful program is obliterated in the museum. In a conception that hearkens back to the Sala degli Imperatori at the Capitoline Museum, the imperial images from the Perge nymphaeum are displayed in a "Hall of Emperors." Those depicting deities stand in a completely separate space in the museum, a "Hall of Gods." Even within those two galleries, the nymphaeum groups are further broken up, their components shuffled in among sculptures from a number of different sites. Installed beside the nymphaeum Zeus, for example, is not the goddess most esteemed at Perge, but rather Zeus' wife, Hera, in the form of a statue from an entirely different city (Aspendos)—a pairing that reveals far more about *our* ideas of the ancient gods than it does about how they were actually lived with or worshipped in antiquity. These statues, as well as those of the emperors in the adjacent gallery (where they are evenly spaced on pedestals or set into architectural niches, with findspot indicated only as "Perge"), have shed all trace of their specific, former affiliations. They have been completely absorbed into the logic of the museum itself. They signify not the statuary ensembles from a handful of particular, complex, well-excavated sites and monuments, but rather the Antalya Museum's large collection of images of Roman gods and Roman emperors. Under such circumstances, the pedagogical and historiographical value of keeping the ensembles at Antalya, rather than allowing their dispersal to collections around the world, is diminished.

Similarly, at the National Archaeological Museum in Athens, the eponymous statue from the so-called House of the Diadoumenos (a large and lavish structure that was in fact probably a businessmen's clubhouse rather than private dwelling) on Delos is featured in the airy, spacious central atrium along with a dozen other sculptures. One of these, a lovely statuette of Artemis, is from the same Delian edifice. It is displayed, however, several statues away from the Diadoumenos. Nothing about the installation indicates any special connection between these two works, and no other works in this space, which include the Horse and Jockey recovered from a shipwreck off Cape Artemesion, and a well-preserved funerary statue of a woman in the "Large Herculaneum" format from the ancient cemetery at Stadiou Street in Athens, have any contextual relation to one another. What they have in common is their status as masterpieces, signalled not only by their central location in the museum, but also by their removal from the archaeological or chronological frameworks that shape the rest of the museum's layout. Meanwhile, the "Pseudo-Athlete," also from the same building on Delos, is on view across the museum in the Roman portrait gallery. Here, one wonders whether a desire to underscore the Greekness of the Diadoumenos and the Artemis (despite the Roman-ness of the findspot and of the associated "Pseudo-Athlete") contributed to the decision to install them in the atrium, rather than preserving the archaeological ensemble.

One could argue, of course, that these museum reconfigurations represent merely the most recent phase in the long "biography" of these objects; that they are appropriations not unlike the appropriation of the mother–daughter statues by some shrewd patron in late antique Aphrodisias (similarly Vout 2012; Squire 2012). I am sympathetic to this argument up to a point. It seems to me, however, that in those relatively rare cases in which we actually do know something about how and with what other objects an artwork was displayed in antiquity, that information deserves to be foregrounded in a museum display. Conversely, for ungrounded artworks like the Fonseca bust or the Munich Marius and Sulla heads, nothing would be more fitting than a display that highlighted their multilayered modern interpretations and meanings.

Less is more

The densely laden visual fields that constituted the original settings of most Roman artworks are discordant with the relatively minimalist, less-is-more installation philosophies that obtain in our museums today (Newhouse 2005). An ensemble of objects in a museum gallery might comprise great works, but their multiplicity denies iconic status to any one of them, especially if, as was often the case in the Roman world, many look quite similar to one another (Trimble 2011, 1–11). Masterpieces are, to the modern mind, lone, unique creations. The modern enthusiasm for single objects, of course, gives further encouragement to dealers to break up looted ensembles and sell their parts off singly. The headless bronze statue of a philosopher, almost certainly Marcus Aurelius and almost certainly plundered in the 1960s from the Antonine sebasteion at Bubon in southern Turkey, would have been part of a riotous display of perhaps 20 bronze and marble imperial statues from that site (Inan and Alföldi-Rosenbaum 1979, 47–8; Chippindale and Gill 2000, 489). It now stands in glorious, spotlit isolation in the center of the Roman gallery at the Cleveland Museum of Art (Fig. 11).

As a general rule of thumb, the more highly an object is esteemed, or the more famous, the more likely it is to be displayed alone, in a spotlit vitrine, atop a stairway landing, at the end of a long architectural vista, in the center of a gallery, or, at the very least, with maximum airspace around it (Vogel 1991). Designed to foster a Greenblattian sense of wonder in the viewer, this installation model might be described as masterpiece theater. An extreme example can be seen at the Archaeological Museum of Volterra. The museum owns many bronze statuettes, often found at Etruscan sanctuaries, depicting extremely elongated human figures. These are displayed in ordinary cases lining the walls of an ordinary gallery, with their votive function

Figure 11   Roman Gallery, Cleveland Museum of Art, featuring the headless bronze statue probably of Marcus Aurelius and probably from Bubon, Turkey.

and associated finds carefully discussed. Nearby, however, in its very own, shadowy gallery, in a dramatically spotlit central case, stands a single ungrounded example of the type, the one known as the "Ombra della Sera" (Evening Shadow). One of the first works to enter the eighteenth-century collection that became the nucleus of the Volterra museum, a whole host of legends has accrued to this figure, from its discovery in the hands of a peasant who was using it as a fire-poker to its popular moniker's invention by the poet Gabrielle D'Annunzio to its influence on the modern Swiss sculptor Alberto Giacometti (Cateni 1998; Gatti and Furiesi 2011; Zevi and Restellini 2011). One can buy a replica of it in almost any size in the giftshop, or dine in half a dozen local restaurants that have been named after it. It is the official emblem of the city of Volterra. The modern fame and local cult of this not-especially-singular object are striking. The museum would have been the ideal venue in which to discuss how, when and why they developed. Instead of a critical discussion, however, the museum only feeds the fire with this shrine-like gallery, and with an extended wall text that extols the perfection of the figure's proportions, the artist's subtle Lysippan influences, and the echoes of its form in the work of Giacometti.

The ungrounded artwork appeals at least in part due to its liberation from the mundane details of its ancient context. James Ackerman suggested that "Works of art of the past are distinguished from political-social acts or artifacts by their capacity to communicate independently of the conditions in and for which they were made" (quoted by Wiseman 1984, 68). It is easier to make the case that an object has achieved this status if we don't know the details of those conditions in the first place. Findspot, associated objects, patrons, and benefactions anchor the object in the particular social or political agendas that motivated its production. Untethered, the work can float free, timeless and universal, a manifestation of pure form, as the ethereal specter of the Ombra della Sera in its darkened gallery amply demonstrates. The less we know, the better.

The modern preference for *less,* for the essence of the thing rather than the thing in all its overladen, multiform abundance, can also be seen in the favoring of disembodied portrait heads over those still attached to their ancient support. In the case of portrait busts—head plus shoulders, chest, "nameplate," and foot, carved from a single block of stone—what we have today is the complete object (Fejfer 2008, 236–61). But many of the ancient portrait heads that have come down to us amount to only half the original work, either because they were broken off at the neck from their original support or because they were carved separately for insertion into a now lost or disassociated herm (a tall pillar often bearing an attribute and/or an inscription) or body (Stewart 2003, 47–59). The bodies usually consisted of generic types that, through pose, costume, and attributes, conveyed the subject's social role (soldier, commander, traveler, Roman citizen, old-fashioned Greek civic benefactor, philosopher, senator, virtuous wife and mother, virginal daughter, etc.) and/or his or her particular virtue (as in the case of Marcus Ulpius Cotronensis, portrayed in the guise of the brave hunter, discussed in Chapter 1) (Niemeyer 1968; Zanker 1989; Smith 1998; Cadario 2011). Complete herms and statues thus present a far richer picture of a portrait's ancient significance than does a free-floating head. But in the pages of handbooks, exhibition catalogs, and scholarly journals, disembodied heads feature far more commonly than complete works (also noted by Stewart 2003, 7–13).

Sometimes the body is devalued even when it is in the very same collection as the head. At the Metropolitan Museum of Art in New York, there is at least one case in which the parts of a single statue are displayed in separate galleries, according to their aesthetic worthiness. A stunning, ungrounded marble portrait head of the Emperor Caracalla is featured in an airy, sparsely appointed room in the museum's new Greek and Roman galleries on the main floor (inv. 40.11.1a) (Fig. 12). The museum believes that two large fragments acquired together with the head in 1940 belong to the lower body of the same figure (inv. 40.11.1b and c). One is a section of the hips and groin, the other a portion of the left leg from mid-shin to just above the knee. The fragments suggest that Caracalla was probably

Figure 12   Gallery 169 of the Greek and Roman collection at the Metropolitan Museum of Art, with marble portrait head of Caracalla, inv. 40.11.1a. Photo by Nancy Gordon.

wearing a short military cuirass, since a toga would have covered his legs. The anatomical details and naturalistic volumes of the knee also provide a contrast to the more abstract geometry of the head. But this comparison, or the general impression of the full statue that the three fragments together could have at least hinted at, cannot be had at the museum. To examine the leg and hips, one must leave Caracalla's gallery, ascend to the mezzanine level, and track them down in the

Figure 13 Case 53, "Roman Sculptural Fragments," in the Greek and Roman Study Collection mezzanine gallery at the Metropolitan Museum of Art. Two fragments of the Caracalla statue (whose head can be seen in Figure 12) are installed on the base at the lower right (40.11.1b and 1c). Photo by Nancy Gordon.

densely packed hall devoted to the Greek and Roman department's "Study Collection." They can be found, unlabeled, in Case 53, "Roman Sculptural Fragments," along with a jumble of other limbs, chins, and fingers from various statues (Fig. 13). To learn what these fragments are, one must key in the number of the case on a touchscreen mounted on the gallery wall.

Indifference to context manifests itself in a variety of ways in Roman art history—in the inconsistencies with which the data is presented in object identifications and captions; in the equal treatment accorded to grounded and ungrounded works; in the frequent neglect of context when it is known; and in the greater attention paid to less complete works than to more complete ones. In the next chapter, I will consider the intellectual consequences of the field's privileging of ungrounded antiquities and the methodology we rely upon to situate them in history, namely, connoisseurship.

3

Lessons Learned and Not Learned

For centuries, art history has relied on connoisseurship to anchor unmoored works to a particular time and place. In the study of European painting and, to a lesser extent, sculpture, this has meant the identification of individual artists' hands. Bernard Berenson quaintly described it as returning lost sheep to their owners, but as he knew well, the practice is one of tremendous financial and historiographical consequence and no less tremendous controversy. It has been the subject of vociferous debate for well over a hundred years. This chapter will consider some of the key points of contention and their relation to Roman art history. My aim here is to offer neither a history nor a particular theory of connoisseurship. It is, rather, to argue that the robust, critical debate surrounding it has endowed later fields of art history with a valuable consciousness of their own epistemology and methodology. Greek art history has also engaged with these questions directly, insofar as recent, mostly Anglophone literature has challenged the traditional focus on named artists and tightly-plotted chronologies of stylistic evolution (e.g. Ridgway 1986, 1994, and 2005; Elsner 1990; Spivey and Rasmussen 1991; Vickers and Gill 1994; Gazda 1995; Moon 1995; Shanks 1996; Palagia and Pollitt 1996; Whitley 2001; Neer 2005; Donohue 2005; Marvin 2008; Osborne 2010).

The Roman field has remained largely outside these debates. This is perhaps due to its looser structure, mostly lacking named artists (although at least one scholar has attempted to identify hands in Pompeiian painting: Richardson 2000) and with far less invested in micro-chronologies. The major stylistic shifts in Roman art history, such as that from the classical to the late antique, for example, have been plotted in terms of centuries or half-centuries rather than decades, as is the case for the shift from Greek archaic to classical. This does not mean, however, that Roman art historians don't practice connoisseurship; they in fact do so every time they situate an ungrounded work in time and space by virtue of its style and formal properties alone. The problem is that this practice is rarely identified, or critically assessed, as connoisseurship; nor is it differentiated from other, less epistemologically shaky uses of formal analysis (exceptions include Smith 2002a; Stewart 2008, 173–6; Scott 2006). Connoisseurship in the Roman field is also sometimes practiced in ways that have been largely rejected among art historians in later fields. These are the subject of this chapter.

Authority and evidence

For much of its early history, connoisseurship was a practice of great men making peremptory pronouncements. The eighteenth-century painter and theorist Jonathan Richardson may have extolled "the science of a connoisseur," but what he meant was that the gentleman-collector, "conversant with the better sort of people, and with the antique," would naturally be able to "judge of the goodness of a picture, of the hand of the master, and whether 'tis an original or a copy" (Richardson 1719; Gibson-Wood 1984 and 2002). With the founding of national public picture galleries in Berlin and London in the nineteenth century, art expertise went from a matter of aristocratic pastime to one of national importance. Connoisseurs such as Wilhelm von Bode, the director of the Staatliche Gemäldegalerie in Berlin (and eventually of the entire Prussian museum system), were prominent national figures and developed towering authority (Scallen 2004). Sir Charles Eastlake, first director of London's National Gallery, defined the connoisseur simply as "he who more especially professes to *know*" rather than to deduce, analyze, or assess (Eastlake 1870, 212, cited by Talley 1989, 184).

This style of connoisseurship by authority was actively challenged in the late nineteenth century by Giovanni Morelli, an Italian doctor and politician (Morelli 1890). Seeking both to debunk the pompous experts and to devise a more rational, deductive method for the attribution of paintings, Morelli offered cheat-sheets with line drawings showing each Renaissance painter's characteristic way of delineating hands and ears (Morelli 1892–3, Vol. 1, 77–8). Armed with such diagnostic tools, the implication was that anyone could test the attributions offered in the gallery labels. Experts such as von Bode and, eventually, Berenson (who was initially a fervent believer in Morelli's method: Berenson 1902) dismissed what they saw as Morelli's mechanistic focus on small details at the expense of larger, more important categories of analysis (Scallen 2004, 89–102). These included quality as well as broad patterns of historical and personal development. These more ineffable traits could only, of course, be discerned by a true connoisseur, a man of rare taste and judgment, who also had the means to travel widely to see original works, not just line drawings (a position endorsed by Talley 1989).

From Morelli on, however, the relationship between instinct and evidence was a matter of much consternation among connoisseurs and their critics. In 1929, the London-based dealer Joseph Duveen was sued for $500,000 by an American couple, Harry and Andrée Hahn, for doubting the attribution of a painting in their possession allegedly by Leonardo da Vinci (Brewer 2009). Duveen made the legitimacy of connoisseurship-by-authority the centerpiece of his defense. Whereas the Hahns' lawyer argued that the case was a matter of "whether the jury shall depend upon the subtle discrimination of an art critic's eye or on the findings of paint chemists on magnified photographs of paint surfaces, and on X-ray examinations of the paint layers below the surface where no art critic's eye can penetrate," Duveen openly scoffed at forensic evidence of any kind (quoted by Brewer 2009, 132). Prominent figures from the international art world lined up behind him. Describing his own abilities as a "sixth sense," Berenson asserted that "When I see a picture … I recognize it at once as being or not being by the master it is ascribed to; the rest is merely a question of how to fish out the evidence that will make the conviction as plain to others as it is to me" (Hahn 1946, 103). Another expert, Maurice Brockwell, explained attributions as a matter "of psychology, not of the magnifying glass; it is the mind of the great master that we see, the spiritual content, the psychological correlations" (quoted by Brewer 2009, 143). While mainstream in the art world, such attitudes translated poorly into the realm of American law. Duveen eventually settled out of court for $60,000. In his opinion of the case, Judge William Harman Black wrote that matters such as "psychological correlations" are "too introspective and subjective to be the basis of any opinion a jury can pin its faith upon" (quoted by Brewer 2009, 145).

Despite this setback, and the even more notorious case of Hans van Meegeren's bogus "Vermeers," which had been embraced by much of the Dutch art establishment, connoisseurship by authority still had its defenders (Lopez 2008). The staunchest was Max Friedländer, the Netherlandish art scholar and Bode's successor as director of the Kaiser Friedrich Museum in Berlin. His 1942 treatise *On Art and Connoisseurship* remains something of a bible among connoisseurs, especially its reassuring chapters about the inevitable triumph of connoisseurship over forgery (e.g. Spencer 2004b, 39–43; Sutton 2007). Friedländer's confidence in expert authority is unabashed: "A picture is shown to me. I glance at it, and declare it to be a work by Memling, without having proceeded to an examination of its full complexity of artistic form. This inner certainty can only be gained from the impression of the whole" (Friedländer 1960 [1942], 173). As for the value of evidence, Friedländer remarks approvingly that, "It is noticeable that gifted experts in particular, who make their decisions with inner certainty, have little inclination to provide 'proof'" (Friedländer 1960 [1942], 167). He goes even further, suggesting derisively that the more evidence presented, the less convincing the attribution: "False attributions are often presented with an excessive display of acuteness, and of arguments which sound irrefutable. False Raphael pictures are accompanied by whole brochures. The weaker the inner certainty, the stronger the need to convince others and oneself by lengthy demonstrations" (Friedländer 1960 [1942], 167).

Despite Friedländer's confidence, the damage had been done. When the Rembrandt Research Project, the largest connoisseurial endeavor of the twentieth century, was launched in 1968, it actively sought to distance itself from the model of connoisseurship by authority. The project aimed to critically re-examine all 613 paintings attributed to Rembrandt in Abraham Bredius' 1935 *catalogue raisonné*, and assign each a grade: "Rembrandt A" (by Rembrandt), "Rembrandt B" (Rembrandt's authorship cannot be positively accepted or rejected), or "Rembrandt C" (not by Rembrandt). Rather than vesting authority in a single, all-powerful expert, attributions would be made by a committee of five. Scientific methods such as dendrochronology, chemical analysis of pigments, and X-ray photography were embraced alongside the analysis of style. The evidence supporting each judgment was to be fully presented and discussed. Finally, the introduction to the first volume (not published until 1982) stated categorically that the committee's findings were to be understood as opinions and not as facts. The Rembrandt Research Project's rejection of connoisseurship by authority became even more radical with the publication of Volume 4, in 2005. The "ABC system" was abandoned entirely, because, as the project's new director, Ernest van de Wetering, acknowledged frankly in the preface, "in many cases no indisputable answer can be given to the question of authenticity. In Volumes I–III the B-category should perhaps have been the largest rather than the smallest" (van de Wetering 2005, xviii; also van de Wetering 2001).

The diagnostic traits Roman art historians rely upon to attribute ungrounded objects have been identified through the visual comparison of one work to another. These traits range from the more deductive, objective, and Morellian—the use of the drill, the depth of drapery folds, the carving of the pupil—to the more expressive, subjective, and/or qualitative, such as the admixture of idealism and verism, or of naturalism and abstract geometry. But it is still common for Roman scholars and curators, in Friedländerisch fashion, to assign ungrounded sculpture to "Italy, first century BCE" or "Asia Minor, second century CE" without naming the stylistic comparanda upon which the hypothesis is based, or even identifying which traits of the object in question have been taken as diagnostic. The attribution is simply asserted, as if it were an irrefutable fact.

One could argue that this practice is not unjustified. Given, for example, how well-documented the prevailing stylistic features of second-century CE sculpture from Asia Minor are (high degree of finish, theatrical contrasts of light and shade, skillful manipulation of a variety of carving tools including the drill, etc.), and how well-known to scholars in the field, one may not feel obliged to itemize them in every case. An attribution may also be a matter of only secondary concern in the context of a larger argument (e.g. about the afterlife, images of foreigners, adaptations of Greek models, luxury, etc.), and so may not seem to be worth distracting detail. In my view, however, neither of these factors counters the inherent epistemological uncertainty endemic to any argument that rests upon ungrounded objects. The onus should always be on the author to *make the case*: to draw attention to what is and isn't known about the object in question, and to lay out the evidence behind his or her attribution so that it can be critically assessed by readers.

The constancy of style

Art historians of previous generations had deep faith in the power of style as a reliable, diagnostic tool (Schapiro 1994 [1953]; Ackerman 1962; Kubler 1962; Gombrich 1968; Bauer 1986; cf. Alpers 1979; Davis 1990; Elsner 2003; Donohue 2005; Pinotti 2012; Borbein 2000 offers a recent defense). Friedländer asserted that an essential, unchanging quality is present in every work by a given artist, who "at bottom remains the same ... something which cannot be lost reveals itself in his every expression" (Friedländer 1960 [1942], 200). He follows this belief to an extreme: "If someone tells me that he owns a Still Life by Frans Hals, signed and dated 1650, I conjure up—without ever having seen a Still Life by Frans Hals—an idea which serves me as a standard as to whether I accept or reject the picture when it is shown to me" (Friedländer 1960 [1942], 176). Having so deeply grasped the essence of Frans Hals, Friedländer believes he can mentally conjure up his own Hals paintings. Likewise Memling: "Somewhat recklessly I venture to claim that we [connoisseurs] learn to paint like Memling, that is, to form the same visions as he. This imaginary pupilage, which naturally has nothing to do with realization—for, of course, we do not become capable of successful forging—obtains for us the inner certainty with which we decide: this must be by Memling, or that cannot be by him" (Friedländer 1960 [1942], 176) (on the proximity of the mental operations of the connoisseur and the forger, see Lenain 2011, 260 and 286).

Connoisseurship on European painting—like much of the discipline of art history and the humanities more broadly—has by now moved beyond such positivism. Explaining the Rembrandt Research Project's abandonment of the ABC system, van de Wetering observes that "historical works of art are complex man-made objects whose materials, manufacture, as well as style and quality can vary even when made by the same person, while on the other hand works that are closely related in just these respects could have been done by different painters" (van de Wetering 2005, xi). In a later publication, he noted that:

> A rigid reliance on familiar characteristics can … end up by dictating, as it were, how Rembrandt should or should not have painted. This sometimes seemed to happen with the old Rembrandt Research Project, precisely because we had pretensions to a scientific approach to connoisseurial judgments … There developed a tendency to force Rembrandt's style and its development into a rational mould, which sometimes led to the de-attribution of paintings that were subsequently decisively shown to be authentic. (van de Wetering 2008, 84)

In the Roman field, however, just such a "rigid reliance on familiar characteristics" continues to guide many attributions of ungrounded artworks (especially, one assumes, those presented without an explicit discussion of their basis). This "rational mould" presumes a steady, consistent, empire-wide evolution of style, iconography (e.g. hairstyles, beards, worried expressions, etc.) and artistic practices, in which the artworks of the imperial capital are almost always taken as the norm. On this model, elderly, veristic portraits are dated to the first century BCE; highly classicizing *Idealplastik* to the Hadrianic era; heavily geometricized forms with exaggerated features to late antiquity, and so on. When applied to objects with no external, supporting evidence, the method is tautological:

- Objects carved in Asia Minor in the second century CE show the use of multiple carving tools and theatrical contrasts between textured surfaces, light and shade, and so forth.
- This object shows those traits.
- Therefore, this object was carved in Asia Minor in the second century CE.

The model excludes the possibility that these formal traits could have been—and would have had reason to be—replicated at other times and places, such as fourth-century Asia Minor, or fifth-century Constantinople, or nineteenth-century Rome. It also assumes that everything produced in Asia Minor in the second century looked that way and not some other way—that there were no workshops that specialized in archaistic works, or no patrons eager to show off an old family connection to, say, the Julio-Claudians, who therefore commissioned an ostentatiously old-fashioned portrait of a grandfather. It allows styles neither to *stick* (whether to particular workshops or to particular social messages) nor to co-exist, to be appropriated, or revived.

In fact, we know that this happened all the time. One of the field's cherished axioms is that what makes Roman art Roman is its multiplicity of styles, and the freedom Roman artists felt to pick and choose according to their subject (Brendel 1979; Hölscher 1987; Smith 1998; Elsner 2004; cf. Kampen 1997). The implications of this fact for dating based on style have been explored by a handful of scholars in recent years. Prosopographical analysis of the inscriptions on a group of Olympian deities found on the Esquiline hill indicates a late antique date, not one in the mid-second century, despite their classicizing style and subject matter (Erim and Roueché 1982; cf. Moltesen 2000). Beards, it turns out, do not necessarily entail a Hadrianic or post-Hadrianic date (Bonanno 1988). R. R. R. Smith has gone further than anyone here, arguing that the great majority of surviving Roman portraits dates to the second century CE; that their formal diversity reflects not stylistic evolution over the course of six centuries, but the diverse social identities of commissioners and the varying self-images they sought to project; and that, in the absence of external, contextual criteria, carving techniques such as drillwork, surface finish, and piecing are the only reliable, formal indicators of date (Smith 1998; Smith et al. 2006, 7–9). Jane Fejfer even doubts the diagnostic value of toolwork for assigning dates (Fejfer 2008, 314–5, on a pair of apparently contemporary statues from the same workshop set up at Cyrene, showing very different handling of the drill).

One of the most tenacious "rational moulds" in Roman art history puts works of greater abstraction and lesser naturalism (and/or simply lesser quality) in late antiquity. This has been challenged along a number of fronts in recent years. Klaus Fittschen as well as Smith have redated a group of "Constantinian" portraits to the second century, based on their carving techniques (Fittschen 1992–3, 463–78 and 1997; Smith 1998, 84). Klaus Parlasca's dating of the painted Fayum portraits according to this model was rejected by Barbara Borg, who offered instead a system based on the imperial hairstyle adopted by the sitter (Borg 1996; Parlasca 1969–80 and 2000; Walker 2000, 34–6; Riggs 2002). This particular node of debate, however, illustrates some of the larger problems facing Roman art historians, particularly those who work with objects lacking external evidence of their specific ancient history. Attributions based on hairstyle would seem to be an improvement over those based on style, if only because the evidence can be more objectively assessed. But one could also argue that one overly broad, rational mould has simply been swapped for another. For Borg, fashion flows directly from the imperial court straight down through provincial and local officials to the ordinary, non-official inhabitants of small communities in Egypt (Borg 1996, 26 and passim). The source of innovation and point of reference is always the ruling couple (especially the empress), never, say, a revered grandmother or high-status woman in a neighboring city or province. Such monolithic and uni-directional models of diffusion have been critiqued by historians rethinking notions of "center and periphery." Scholars such as Greg Woolf, David Mattingly, and Sarah Scott, as well as Smith, have emphasized instead the diverse array of local models and concerns that shaped all aspects of cultural production at the local level (a good overview can be found in Scott 2003). There is also hard evidence suggesting that the popularity of any given coiffure could outlast the empress who'd made it fashionable, and that Roman women enjoyed an array of styling options at any given moment. A woman who died in the eruption of Vesuvius, whose body cast now resides in the Pompeii Antiquarium, was still wearing the *nodus* hairstyle popularized by the Empress Livia over half a century earlier (illustrated in Coates et al. 2012, 219n. 79; I thank Elaine Gazda and Barbara Kellum for this observation). A group of marble portrait dedications at the Sanctuary of Diana at Nemi, once assigned a range of individual, first-century dates based on their diverse hairstyles, have recently been shown, through isotopic analysis, to belong to a single dedication (Fejfer 2008, 305; contra Moltesen 1997, 144). Freedmen's group portrait reliefs regularly show multiple female family members each sporting a different hairstyle (Buccino 2011, 368). That a middle-class woman in a remote Egyptian town would choose to have herself depicted with the same intricate hairstyle popularized by Agrippina Minor can shed light on questions of class, identity, and "Romanization." But its reliability as a dating tool is less absolute than we would like it to be.

There are even more extreme cases in the Roman historiography where broad assumptions about the constancy of period style have outweighed other evidence and historical considerations. At the Metropolitan Museum of Art, for example, resides an ungrounded, over-life-sized, nude bronze portrait statue purchased by the museum in 1905 (Fitz Gerald 1905; McCann 1981; Picón et al. 2007, 497–8,

Figure 14   Bronze portrait statue conventionally identified as "Trebonianus Gallus,"
Metropolitan Museum of Art, inv. 05.30. Findspot unknown. First attested in the
collection of Auguste de Montferrand in St. Petersburg in 1849, who claimed that it had
been excavated by the Russian Count Nicolas Demidoff near the Lateran in Rome in
the early nineteenth century. Sold by Montferrand's heirs in 1870 to the Paris dealers
Rollin and Feuardent, who sold it to the Metropolitan Museum in 1905. Image © The
Metropolitan Museum of Art.

cat. no. 471; Marlowe forthcoming) (Fig. 14). Since its arrival at the
museum, it has been identified as Trebonianus Gallus (r. 251-3 CE),
a "soldier-emperor" from the mid-third century period of Rome's
military anarchy. The figure's awkward contrapposto, heavy torso,
tiny head, and contorted facial muscles, however, are unique in the
corpus of Roman portrait statuary. The lack of comparanda, and the
figure's seemingly unhonorific qualities, could perhaps indicate that
the statue portrayed someone other than an emperor (such as an
athlete, an identification for which comparanda do exist). The imperial
identification rests primarily on the figure's buzzed haircut and stubble
beard, which also feature on coin portraits of the soldier-emperors
(the drapery and possibly the shoes as well are modern restorations). Many of those coin images also display a noticeable disregard
for naturalistic forms, favoring simple planes and geometric shapes
instead. Extrapolating from the coins, as well as from literary descriptions of the soldier-emperors as "cruel" and "depraved," scholars seem
to have developed a mental picture of what a whole portrait-statue of
a soldier-emperor *should* have looked like—just as Friedländer moved
from actual Hals paintings to ones Hals never actually painted. The
military look and unclassical style of the Metropolitan's 8-foot-tall
statue conforms to that picture (see further discussion of this statue in
Chapter 4).

Hypotheses built upon hypotheses

One reason for the Rembrandt Research Project's abandonment of
the ABC system was the recognition that, "Through all phases of
Rembrandt's career the essential core of his oeuvre cannot be demar-
cated with certainty ... In short, it is unclear to what extent the core
group of works to which the connoisseur intuitively refers is in fact
'contaminated' by mistaken attributions" (van de Wetering 2008, 84; see
also Beck 1998 and 2006, 32-3). Even Friedländer urged caution: "One
should always avoid as far as possible to link up an attribution based on

style-criticism with another such attribution—in other words, to forge chains—since, of course, the risk of mistake is always there, and steps must be taken in advance to ensure that error does not produce error. A return to the secure starting-point remains imperative, to a centre from which attributions issue like rays" (Friedländer 1960 [1942], 175). Many ungrounded works of Roman art, however, have been identified or interpreted based on affinities with other ungrounded objects. I have already noted the head in Fiesole, whose anomalies (particularly the alabaster medium) have presumably been overlooked because of its close affinity with the Fonseca bust. Epistemological incaution also undermines Wolf-R. Megow's recent catalog of Republican portraits (Megow 2005). The catalog identifies 15 major types, into which 83 specimens are sorted as replicas. Only 16 of the 83 are grounded, and six of the 15 types are attested only by ungrounded replicas. This is not a secure corpus upon which to build an understanding of ancient portraiture.

Similarly, Luca Giuliani's 1986 monograph on Republican portraiture offered a theory about the emergence and ideological significance of the veristic style in the late Republic based on a set of objects—ostensibly pre-Sullan, second-century BCE "pathos" portraits—for which there is not a single securely dated example (Giuliani 1986; also noted by Smith 1988b). Indeed, his primary exemplars of the style are the so-called Marius and Sulla portraits in Munich (which he identifies as Augustan copies of second-century BCE portraits of unidentified, leading men), whose many epistemological uncertainties were discussed in Chapter 2 (Giuliani 1986, 175–88). Giuliani's other main case study is the head of Pompey in Copenhagen (Giuliani 1986, 67–72). This object is not ungrounded, but it is grounded in the first century CE, not BCE. These works constitute shaky ground upon which to construct an entire theory about the emergence of the veristic style.

One of the tallest houses of cards in Roman art historiography has been built atop the Barberini Togatus (Fig. 15). The life-sized statue depicts a togate male (whose head is not original to this statue), wearing *calceii patricii* (short, senatorial boots with crossing straps)

Figure 15   Marble statue known as the Barberini Togatus, Capitoline Museum at Montemartini, inv. 2392. Findspot unknown. First attested in the Barberini collection in 1627, where it is recorded as a gift from Filippo Colonna to Cardinal Francesco Barberini. Acquired by the Capitoline Museum in 1937.

and cradling a portrait bust of an elderly man in either hand; one bust rests on a tall, date-palm pedestal. The statue is routinely deployed in the historiography as the hermeneutic key to the whole genre of Roman portraiture; Jean-Charles Balty's short monograph on "portraiture and society in the Roman world," for example, features the work as its frontispiece (Balty 1991). The latest catalog of the Capitoline Museum at Montemartini, the statue's current home, explains that the work displays "the high social rank" of a patrician family, both through his toga and through the "images of ancestors" he bears. The catalog continues: "The custom of making figures of ancestors in wax was ... reserved only for aristocratic families who kept them in the hall of the house and 'wore' them at special public and private events so that their ancestors would also be present" (Bertoletti et al. 1998, 53). The text here refers to the wax *imagines* known from ancient literary sources. Polybius tells us that after a funeral:

> [Romans] place a likeness of the dead man in the most public part of the house, keeping it in a small wooden shrine. The likeness is a mask especially made for a close resemblance both as regards the shape of the face and its coloring. They open these masks during public sacrifices and compete in decorating them. And whenever a leading member of the family dies, they introduce them into the funeral procession, putting them on men who seem most like them in height and as regards the rest of their general appearance. (*Histories* 6.53.4–7; translation Flower 1996, 309)

Likewise, Pliny notes that:

> In... the atria of the ancestors ... portraits offered a spectacle to behold, not the statues by foreign artists either of bronze or of marble; but faces rendered in wax were arranged in separate cupboards, so that they should be "true portraits'" (*imagines*) to accompany funerals in the extended family. (*Natural History*, 35.6; translation Flower 1996, 304)

Since at least the 1930s, art historians have read the Barberini Togatus busts in light of the patrician *imagines* (Zadoks-Josephus Jitta 1932,

45). They have been eager to see the statue as the otherwise missing link between that institution and the production of veristic portraiture (e.g. Lahusen 1985; Pollini 2007, with additional bibliography). The obvious mismatch between wearable wax masks and the heavy stone heads hand-carried by the Togatus has been explained away through various means, such as the scare-quotes around the word "wore" in the Montemartini catalog cited above (on the mismatch, see Flower 1996, 5–6). One recent formulation states that "They are not, however, wax *imagines*, because they are sculptures in the round, not masks. The statue nonetheless would have had the same effect on the observer as the spectacle of parading ancestors at a patrician funeral" (Kleiner 2010, 52).

The problem, however, is that we have no idea where this ungrounded statue would have been displayed in the ancient world. The statue's "effect on the observer" would have depended greatly on the context in which he or she beheld it: patrician villa peristyle? freedman's household atrium? public square in a provincial Italian town? tomb façade on a road leading into Rome? tomb interior? Art historians have used literary descriptions of patrician ancestral parades as a sort of quasi-context for this statue, but this is in fact a case where our ignorance of the work's physical setting is particularly detrimental (also noted by Fittschen 2006a, 173; Picozzi 2010, 54 on a possible zone of recovery; Lavin 1975, 78–9 on the Barberini documents). The Barberini Togatus is not an ancestor portrait; it is a life-sized statue of a man *holding ancestor portraits*. It does not partake of that deeply rooted aristocratic institution; rather, it is *about* that institution, self-consciously thematizing it. Mathias Hofter argued influentially that the statue depicts either a *novus homo* or a municipal magistrate, neither of whom would have been permitted to hold an actual, grand, *imagines*-filled funeral (Hofter 1988, 341–2; on municipal magistrates: Zanker 1983). "Yearning to emulate the practice on a smaller scale," they settled for this mini version, an "abbreviated ancestor portrait gallery," (La Rocca et al. 2011, 46; Hofter 1988, 342, respectively). The character of the striving *arriviste* who apes the practices of his social betters is one well-familiar to aristocrats both ancient and modern (viz. Trimalchio, Gatsby, the Rodney Dangerfield character in *Caddyshack*, etc.). It is also one assumed by much of the historiography on Roman art, as will be discussed in Chapter 4. Whether the ancient middle classes actually behaved this way or would have invested considerable sums of money to commemorate their position *just outside* traditional aristocratic norms (as, according to this reading, the Barberini Togatus does), is another question (see Mayer 2012 for a lucid critique of these assumptions). My point here is that with no information about its findspot, this statue, far from offering a hermeneutic key to the institution of Roman portraiture, raises more questions than it answers.

A quick final observation here. There is, of course, no doubt that the veneration of ancestors was a primary function of Roman portraiture. To illustrate that fact, a more compelling and epistemologically stable example than the Barberini Togatus is the famous portrait of Pompey in Copenhagen. The head was installed in the family tomb by Pompey's descendants, along with over a dozen other portraits ranging in date from the Augustan period to the mid-second century. (Reports about the findspot are contradictory and compromised, but a recent, thorough archival study affirms the basic facts about the group: Kragelund et al. 2003, 81–100; cf. van Keuren 2003.) Seen as a retrospective construction of the first century CE, rather than as a necessarily faithful reflection of Pompey's portraiture during his lifetime, the head, and its idiosyncratic features, look somewhat different. It is probably no coincidence that both the sculpted portrait and Plutarch's verbal portrait of Pompey emphasize his boyish charm and his dramatic, Alexander-like *anastole* (Plutarch, *Life of Pompey*, 2). Both projections underscore the traits for which, a century or a century and a half later, Pompey was most remembered. Both, in other words, exaggerate his essential Pompey-ness.

In the wonderful 2006 reinstallation of the Tomb of the Licinii ensemble at the Ny Carlsberg Glyptotek in Copenhagen, Pompey is framed by a series of portraits showing the features and wearing the hairstyles of many subsequent generations. This makes it easy to appreciate the head as an ancient, venerated ancestor of a distinguished, long-lived family clan. The ensemble also, incidentally, reveals the prominent role of women in such constructed family trees (Boschung 1986; Kragelund 2002). This well-displayed, grounded group of portraits offers a firm foundation from which to examine the role of portraiture in Roman society.

The art market

During the "age of connoisseurship" (Schwartz 1995), the value of an expert's opinion was predicated upon his unimpeachable integrity. Meyer Schapiro hastened the end of that age with a scathing article about Bernard Berenson published shortly after Berenson's death in 1959 (Schapiro 1961; Simpson 1986; Olin 1994). Schapiro drew attention to the 25 percent cut Berenson had secretly been earning on paintings sold with his authentication. In fact, it is impossible to disentangle connoisseurship from the art market, given the value collectors attach to certain names and the need for experts to sanction them. One can only hope that conflicts of interest will be openly acknowledged. (In his 1921 publication of "Rediscovered [Rembrandt] Paintings," Wilhelm Valentiner cheerily acknowledged that "the urge to research and the pursuit of gain went hand in hand"; cited in Schwartz 1995, 319.)

Today, the practice of connoisseurship in later areas of art history is associated primarily with the market rather than with academia (Tancock 2004). Relatively few university course offerings, conference sessions or publications are devoted to the topic. On its website, the Catalogue Raisonné Scholars Association, a professional organization of connoisseurs, identifies its audience as "patrons, collectors, art dealers, attorneys, and software designers." It is composed largely of independent scholars, curators, and employees of artists' estates; only 12 percent of its members' contact information indicates an academic affiliation.

In the Roman field, however, the lines are blurrier. In their routine use of connoisseurship to incorporate ungrounded objects into historical narratives, Roman art historians in the academy share—and legitimize—the intellectual premises of those invested in the ancient art market. Dealers market ungrounded, possibly looted, or possibly forged antiquities to buyers not just as beautiful objects but also as relics of the Roman past, whose place in history the dealer ensures through connoisseurship. Their methods and assumptions differ only in two ways. One is that the scholar is presumably not being directly remunerated for his or her attributions. The other is that he or she could choose not to work with ungrounded objects, whereas dealers, in most cases, have no choice, due to various laws governing the market in antiquities.

I emphasize the legitimizing affinities between scholarly practices and those of the market because, in the recent, super-heated rhetoric on looting, the complicity of academia has been largely overlooked (Muscarella 2000 and 2009 are exceptions). Instead, the blame has been placed squarely on buyers, since looting is predicated upon a robust market. As Ricardo Elia and Colin Renfrew put it bluntly, "collectors are the real looters" (Elia 1993, 69; Renfrew 1993). Indeed, since the Metropolitan Museum of Art's purchase of the Euphronios krater in 1972, and the outcry it triggered, the discourse around looting has pitted archaeologists against collectors and, by extension, academics against museums (Dyson 1998, 277–81; Bauer 2008). When it entered the collection in 1972, the vase was the museum's highest priced antiquity. Director Thomas Hoving called it "one of the two or three finest works ever gained by the Metropolitan," one that will require "histories of art to be rewritten" (Hoving 1972). It was featured in color on the cover of the *New York Times'* Sunday Magazine. Very quickly, however, the museum's official story of the vase's ownership history (that it had been in a private Lebanese collection since 1920) began to crumble, replaced by rumors that it had been plundered quite recently from a cemetery in Cerveteri. At the height of the controversy, Dietrich von Bothmer, the museum's curator of Greek and Roman art, gave a paper on the krater at the annual meeting of the Archaeological Institute of America. As a result, he was blocked in his bid for a seat on the organization's board (Shirey 1973; Silver 2009, 76–9). The Institute then passed its first resolution condemning the trade in undocumented antiquities and calling upon all members, both individuals and institutions, to follow the strictures of the new UNESCO Convention. The Institute also formulated a policy against serving as the initial venue for the presentation of newly surfaced objects, subsequently the basis for the editorial policy adopted by the *American Journal of Archaeology* against publishing such objects as well (Kleiner 1990; Kyrieleis 2000; Norman 2005) (more on this policy, as well as the UNESCO Convention, in Chapter 4).

The episode opened up a seemingly irrevocable breach between the academy and the museum world over the issue of recently-surfaced antiquities. In 1999, for example, the two sides squared off over a gold phiale, said to have been looted from Italy, in the collection of hedge fund manager Michael Steinhardt. The American Association of Museums and the Association of Art Museum Directors spoke on the collector's behalf, while the American Institute of Archaeology, the Society for American Archaeology, the American Anthropological Association, and the Society for Historical Archaeology took an opposing position (the phiale was eventually handed over to Italian authorities) (Gerstenblith 2003). The 2004 Italian conviction of Giacomo Medici for trafficking in illegal antiquities tipped the balance decisively against the museums. It resulted not only in the return of more than 140 objects from various public and private collections (including the Euphronios krater), but also in the sensational Rome trial of former Getty Museum curator Marion True on charges of conspiring to traffic in antiquities looted from Italian soil (Watson and Todeschini 2006; Mead 2007; Godart and de Caro 2007; Gill 2009; Felch and Frammolino 2011; Bell 2011).

In contrast to the opprobrium heaped upon the museum world in recent years, the practices of university-based scholars of ancient art, removed from the taint of the market, have not come under close scrutiny. Most of the academics who have actively engaged with the issues have spoken out against the trade in antiquities, urging the United States to sign or renew Memoranda of Understanding with various nations to uphold their cultural patrimony laws (as per the UNESCO Convention); testifying against dealers such as Frederick Schultz; publicly debating with Metropolitan Museum director Philippe de Montebello; writing blistering reviews of James Cuno's many declarations of museums as the saviors of cultural heritage; and explaining the connection between the market and the destruction of sites on blogs, in letters to the editors of major newspapers, and in many professional publications. These are valuable contributions to the conversation. The next step, in my view, will be to pay greater critical attention to the ways in which academics handle ungrounded antiquities—and not just those that surfaced after 1970—in our scholarship and teaching. If scholars were more insistent and consistent about the importance of external data in historicizing an artwork, it would throw the shaky foundations of connoisseurship into greater relief. This might at least partly destabilize some of the basic working assumptions of the art market and might even discourage potential buyers. But as long as both scholars and dealers offer an uncritical, uncomplicated version of history-through-connoisseurship, the method will retain its legitimacy, and ungrounded antiquities their value. Unlike in later fields of art history, where the compromising connections between connoisseurship and the market have been fully exposed, Roman art history has yet to critically examine the implications of its own connoisseurial practices.

Connoisseurship and Class

Social art history

The previous chapter argued that connoisseurship in Roman art history is sometimes practiced with less self-awareness than connoisseurship in other art historical fields. One still encounters attributions made without supporting evidence, assumptions about monolithic and steadily-evolving styles, and hypotheses built upon hypotheses, while critical reflection on the relationship between scholarly practices and the market is relatively rare. Another difference is that scholars of later art historical periods also tend to see fundamental incompatibilities between connoisseurship, on the one hand, and what can broadly be described as "social art history," on the other.

In one of the earliest manifestoes against connoisseurship, published in the *Times Literary Supplement*, T. J. Clark drew upon an older, explicitly Marxist tradition associated with Frederick Antal and Arnold Hauser. Clark called upon art historians to shift their attention away from their "narrow, taxonomic focus on the identification of individual artists' hands," and toward "the relation between the work of art and its ideology," defined as "those bodies of beliefs, images, clues and techniques of representation by which social classes, in conflict with each other, attempt to 'naturalize' their particular histories" (Clark 1974).

From Clark's rallying cry emerged what came to be known first as the "new art history" (e.g. Borzello and Rees 1986), which evolved into "visual culture" during the 1990s (e.g. Cartwright and Sturken 2001; Herbert 2003; Corbett 2005). Notions of "identity" are often foregrounded in related literature today (Meyer 2003; Bell and Hansen

2008). One feature these various, newer methodological committ-
ments share is their strong repudiation of connoisseurship; indeed,
connoisseurship serves as a sort of "other" against which those who
practice these methods define themselves (Clunas 2003). As Richard
Neer recently put it, "It is difficult to overstate the ill repute in which
connoisseurship now stands among all but the most hidebound archaeologists and art historians; it has been the defining scapegoat of both
disciplines for the last twenty years and more" (Neer 2005, 2). Most
scholars of Roman art would, I believe, be quick to align themselves
with the social art historians. This chapter considers the ways in which
reliance on ungrounded objects undermines that position.

Hints of Marxist priorities first appeared in Roman art historiography with Ranucchio Bianchi Bandinelli's valorization of "plebeian
art" in 1967, followed by Paul Zanker's 1975 study of the funerary
reliefs of freedmen (Bianchi Bandinelli 1967; Zanker 1975). In the
1980s came a wave of studies that turned away from traditional
subjects such as the sequence of imperial portrait typologies and
Kopienkritik (the identification of lost Greek originals through Roman
replicas). These publications considered instead the self-fashioning
of various social groups through images and monuments: from the
emperor (MacCormack 1981; Zanker 1988) and late Republican aristocrats (Giuliani 1986) to provincial elites (Price 1984), the working
middle classes (Kampen 1981; Zimmer 1982); and, in the 1990s,
middle-class Campanian home-owners (Wallace-Hadrill 1994) and
wealthy villa-owners (Bergmann 1995; for a good historiographical
overview, see Stewart 2008, 173–6 and passim). The basic premises
of social art history, with its focus on viewers and patrons, have been
broadly embraced by the field, particularly its Anglophone branches.
This is evident most recently in the increasing number of publications devoted to topics such as spolia (Kinney and Brilliant 2011, with
previous bibliography), freedmen (Clarke 2003; Petersen 2006; Mayer
2012), provincial art (Scott and Webster 2003; D'Ambra and Métraux
2006), and, more broadly, "identity" (Bell and Hansen 2008; Hales and
Hodos 2010).

With the important exception of the literature on provincial art, however, ungrounded antiquities continue to feature in much of this new historiography. In interpreting such objects, these studies necessarily fall back on generic or conventional wisdom about types and styles, rather than analyzing specific data about the works' commissioners, architectural frame, grouping with other works, use, or reuse. Some of the methodological inconsistencies can perhaps be understood as signs of a discipline in transition. In an astute essay on Roman art historiography, R. R. R. Smith contrasts the older, artist-based approach and the newer, patron-and-viewer-centric orientation (Smith 2002a). He advocates forcefully for the advantages of the latter, observing that, "At the moment most scholars ... combine them in an unselfconscious, untheorised way according to intellectual taste, the questions chosen and the evidence available" (Smith 2002a, 73).

Smith is right, but his essay itself inadvertently illustrates these very contradictions. He speaks enthusiastically about the "new material" in the area of imperial portraiture that is "constantly fill[ing] out and expand[ing] the picture" (Smith 2002a, 92). But as an example he cites not a portrait discovered in some telling ancient context but rather a gilded bronze head of Nero that recently surfaced in a private German collection (Born and Stemmer 1996). He expresses no regret for the piece's lost findspot, which might have explained—among other things—how this despised ruler's portrait, bluntly severed from its body in antiquity, escaped the flames (Eric Varner wonders if it was "ritually buried"; Varner 2004, 70). The essay's rousing conclusion proclaims the unique power of ancient images to show us how ancient peoples saw themselves. Smith illustrates the point with an ungrounded limestone funerary relief of a Palmyrene woman, who is "definitively constituted by a striking combination of exaggerated ideal Hellenic beauty and a rich jewelry-encrustation that belongs to pre-classical and local traditions" (Smith 2002a, 99). But as Smith's own work at Aphrodisias has so powerfully demonstrated, what would have "definitively constituted" her is the complete tomb ensemble to which her image originally belonged. Whether or not her beauty would have struck the viewer as "exaggerated," "ideal," or "Hellenic," would surely have been inflected by how the other figures in the (now lost) surrounding reliefs were portrayed. Instead of an isolated Palmyrene relief "from the art market in New York," Smith's important point about ancient self-fashioning might have been more persuasively made with an example whose ancient environment has been preserved, such as one of the many portrait-reliefs from the Hypogeum of Yarhai, magnificently reconstructed in the crypt of the National Museum in Damascus (Amy and Seyrig 1936; Gabucci 2002, 81–2; for another example, see Schmidt-Colinet et al. 1992).

The reliance on ungrounded artworks can undermine the objectives of social art history. We can generalize broadly about the style of such objects, but we cannot shift the focus from artists to patrons and users if we have no data external to the object itself by which to assess its forms. Forms alone are a record of *what* a particular artist did; to understand *why* he did it, whose needs those forms served, requires information about where an object was displayed, who commissioned it, what ensemble it belonged to, or how it was subsequently deployed. After all, even if we have correctly diagnosed from careful stylistic analysis that a work was created in Asia Minor in the second century, what have we learned? Aphrodisian sculpture was exported all over the empire. Identifying place and date of manufacture tells us little about how and where an object was used.

Circular logic

In fact, some of what might, at first glance, look like social art history in the Roman field appears, upon closer examination, to fall into an odd, in-between category, in which style-based attributions of date (connoisseurship) and interpretations of social significance are locked in tautological circles. Ungrounded objects are assigned to certain times, places and patrons based on their formal similarity to other objects produced there, then, and for those people. The interests and ideology of those groups are then read back into the objects' forms, thus apparently confirming the attribution. The possibility that *other* patrons at different times or places might have deployed the same forms to communicate their own messages is excluded *a priori*. As David Ebitz once noted approvingly, "there must be internal coherence, a comfortable fit for a new attribution, for example, within an existing hypothesis concerning the development of an artist ... When the attribution fits, and the hypothesis works, there is a sense of rightness that has the feel of truth" (Ebitz 1988, 210). This is a comforting notion. If we think an ungrounded funerary relief is, say, late antique, because it looks like what we think a late antique relief of its type would look like, then the attribution will have a sufficient "sense of rightness" and "feel of truth." We can call the relief late antique.

One could also argue, however, that connoisseurship's self-affirming structure is one of its great dangers. As Christopher Chippindale and David Gill have argued, attributions of ungrounded ancient artworks can only

> confirm, reinforce, and strengthen the existing patterns of knowledge. Surfacing without secure information beyond what is immanent in themselves, the objects are unable to broaden our basis of knowledge. Interpreted and restored in light of prior expectations, they are reconciled with what we presently know, but they cannot amend and improve our present knowledge much, if at all (Chippindale and Gill 2000, 504–5).

By design, connoisseurial attributions of ungrounded artworks cannot surprise us, or challenge our preconceived ideas. Only grounded works, whose forms can be read in light of reliable, external data, can do that. This happened in dramatic fashion in the Greek field, with the discovery of a life-sized marble figure probably representing a charioteer at the Punic site of Mozia, a small island off the west coast of Sicily (Bonacasa and Buttuita 1988; Bell 1995; Lapatin 2000). Meticulous formal analysis of the statue identified an astonishing combination of styles: a restrained, "severe"-style head (typical of the early fifth century

BCE); a brash, thrusting pose comparable to the expressive, "baroque" attributes associated with the Hellenistic period; and a sensuous, virile body sheathed in sheer, densely pleated, clingy fabric, which has no sculpted parallel in the ancient world. The Mozia charioteer defied conventional wisdom about both Greek sculpture and Punic culture. As one scholar noted shortly after its discovery, many "feel embarrassed by its peculiarities, by the strangeness of the work, especially if one compares it to the Greek works that one takes to be 'normal'" (Dontas 1988, 61). Had the Charioteer first surfaced on the art market, its uniqueness and apparent discrepancy of styles would likely have been seen as indicative of either a Roman pastiche (thereby sending Romanists off on a wild goose chase to find a plausible social context for it) or a modern forgery (Fuchs 1988, 79). Instead, its recovery in a controlled context not only proves its antiquity but gives us a terminus ante quem of 397 BCE, for it was found in a level that pre-dates the destruction of Mozia by Syracuse in that year. The combination of the Mozia Charioteer's style and findspot changed our understanding of ancient art and cultural interactions. We now know that Greek sculptural styles were more diverse and appropriated more widely than had previously been recognized; and that the sharp line we instinctively draw between "Greek" and "Punic" could actually be a relatively fluid one (e.g. Bisi 1988, 69). "Stupefied by the statue's novelty" (di Vita 1988, 39), scholars were forced to broaden their narrow taxonomies and expectations (Lapatin 2000, 46).

Revolutions happen more slowly in the Roman field. Despite the work of Smith and Bonanno cited in Chapter 3, for example, Hadrian's beard is still taken as a fixed line in the sand in the dating of ungrounded male portraits. Eventually, however, exceptions accumulate and rules are revised. Enough classicizing pagan mythological statuettes have been discovered in late antique villas, for example, and enough publications have trumpeted their significance that older assumptions about Christianity and an ostensibly abrupt end of the classical tradition have been laid to rest (Erim and Roueché 1982; Hannestad 1994; Bergmann 1999; Moltesen 2000; Stirling 2005) (note, by contrast, the to-our-eyes-striking absence of such material in the Metropolitan Museum's *Age of Spirituality* catalog; Weitzmann 1979). Such paradigm shifts occur only when external evidence, such as archaeological context or artists' signatures, breaks the circle of our mutually reinforcing assumptions about forms, dates, and social significance.

Contrast such happy outcomes with the fate of prominent ungrounded objects, such as the Metropolitan Museum's so-called Trebonianus Gallus statue, discussed briefly in the previous chapter (Picón et al. 2007, 497–8). Like the Mozia Charioteer in that it departs radically from classical norms (albeit in different ways), this figure has had the opposite effect on our understanding of the ancient world. Rather than overturning narrow taxonomies and preconceptions, it has reinforced them. The statue's identification was based on soldier-emperors' coins, but its contorted expression and ungainly body also dovetailed nicely with the modern view of such men: "There can be no doubt that the subject is the notorious Trebonianus Gallus, the degenerate Roman of the third century, who is chiefly remembered for the dishonourable peace he made with the Goths upon the death of his predecessor, Trajanus Decius" (Mather 1905, 148). In 1977, the statue was the first item featured in the Metropolitan's influential exhibit, "The Age of Spirituality: Late Antique and Early Christian Art," where its "harsh linear surface detail" and "distorted" brow were emphasized (Weitzmann 1979, 8–9). Since then, it has served as a linchpin in arguments connecting the demise of the classical style to the decline of the old, senatorial aristocracy and the concomitant rise of a new class of military leaders. In 1981, one scholar observed that, "The classical Greek philosopher model still so clearly behind the portrait image of Marcus Aurelius in Indiana has been completely abandoned for an anti-rational and anti-classical portrayal of the military rule" in this statue (McCann 1981, 632). The class connotations are spelled out even more explicitly in a recent textbook:

> In the era of the soldier emperors, this new kind of ideal body type began to be used in place of the Classical Greek type for imperial portraits ... This was, after all, an age in which a barbarian of low birth

... could become emperor almost solely on the basis of his physical size and strength. (Kleiner 2010, 268)

The statue is paired here with a lengthy quotation from the biography of the emperor Maximinus Thrax in the *Historia Augusta*. This collection of imperial biographies was written pseudonymously, but historical and philological clues suggest authorship by a late fourth-century, metropolitan-Rome-based aristocrat (Chastagnol 1994; Thomson 2012, with earlier bibliography). The text reveals the deep hostility with which these patricians remembered the military commanders who had taken over the governance of the empire a century earlier, starting with Maximinus (whose troops had murdered the last scion of the Severan family) (Moralee 2008). The selected passage emphasizes Maximinus' barbarity, illiteracy, and intimidating physical stature. The textbook implies a causal relationship between these traits and the statue's unconventional forms: these men were this way, and that's what the portrait shows. The figure, with its massive, intimidating scale, incorrect contrapposto, and uncouth scowl, represents a crude, illiterate, physically intimidating third-century soldier-emperor. The style proves the meaning, which proves the date, which determines the style. Such circularity of interpretation, untethered to any secure facts, is inevitable for ungrounded objects.

The problem with this reading of the Metropolitan bronze is that it takes the outlook of the disgruntled, reactionary fourth-century elites, writing a century after the fact, as the uncomplicated truth. It also ignores the fact that portrait statuary was erected in the Roman world for honorific purposes. Would anyone's interests have been served by sponsoring an image of a ruler that emphasized his "troubled psyche" (Kleiner 2010)? These issues have not been explored in the literature, nor has the possibility that the statue might represent anyone other than a soldier-emperor. The standard interpretation of the Metropolitan statue affirms entrenched ideas about late antique artistic and cultural decline as the consequence of a sort of military-proletarian class revolution. It also reinforces the belief that differences between men of "low birth" and men of high birth are ontological, inescapable, and written in visible ways on their bodies, no matter how high up the political ladder they may climb; and that one's proximity to classical traditions is an essential axis of class differentiation. Such notions no doubt comforted the indignant aristocrats of late antique Rome, but warrant critical unpacking today.

Empty niches

The same circular logic that makes the Metropolitan bronze a third-century soldier-emperor, thus proving that the classical style declined because emperors now came from the military classes rather than from the aristocracy, is evident elsewhere in the historiography of Roman art. A recent monograph argues that certain scene types that appear on sarcophagi (e.g. battles, marriages, and hunts) would only have been appropriate for (or appealing to) senators, and so must have been produced for members of that social class (Wrede 2001). The author then proceeds to interpret the values and concerns of the senatorial class over time based on the relative prominence of those particular scenes. The argument, however, is circular (as noted by Ewald 2003, 563; Kleiner 2003; Fejfer 2008, 466n. 132). It cannot be ruled out, for example, that some of these sarcophagi may have been used by (and even produced for) wealthy freedmen (Kleiner 2003).

Perhaps the most enduring historiographic tradition built upon mutually reinforcing connoisseurship and ostensibly social art history is the literature on veristic portraiture. A recent catalog compiled 330 examples of these male heads, characterized by their emphasis on the signs of age, particularly toothless gums, balding pates, and lined, sagging skin (Croz 2002). Although only a very small handful can be dated on external evidence, the genre has always been associated with the patricians of the late Republican period. Much of the historiography is concerned with assembling replica groups and identifying the sitters as famous figures from late Republican history (the practice begins with Bernoulli 1882 and continues through Megow 2005). In this regard, it resembles the literature on imperial portrait typologies, but, given the absence of securely dated and identified coin types, its evidential basis is significantly weaker (for critical discussions of this literature, see Vessberg 1941; Ridgway 1986, 13; Gazda and Haeckl 1993, 299–302; Fejfer 2008, 4–7).

These ungrounded portraits have played a prominent role in the social art history of Republican Rome—which in turn appears to affirm the assumption about their dates. Since the 1930s the style has been linked to the patrician practice of parading wax masks of deceased family members—presumably equally unidealized—at public ceremonies (briefly discussed in Chapter 3; Zadoks-Josephus Jitta 1932; Drerup 1980; Flower 1996, 53–9 and passim; Pollini 2007; contra Rose 2008, 112–5). This right was exclusive to the descendants of those who had attained curule status. Scholars of the post-war decades saw the style as an expression of reactionary ideology against the populist reforms of the Gracchi (Bianchi Bandinelli 1970, 77–9); against Hellenistic rulers (Smith 1988a, 128–80); or against the dictatorship of Sulla (Giuliani 1986, 200–20). More broadly, and influentially, Luca Giuliani connected the veristic style's ostentatious display of advanced age with the conservative seno-philia of Republican society, a geron-tocracy whose values, such as *gravitas, constantia,* and *severitas,* are celebrated in the rhetoric of Cicero (Giuliani 1986, 195 and 200–38). Today there is consensus that the style emphasizes the class solidarity and shared values of the late Republican aristocracy.

At the same time, however, the understanding of the social signifi-cance of verism has broadened in the past few decades, as scholars have turned their attention to reliefs honoring mid-level Italian magistrates, freedmen, and the working classes, where the style is also prevalent. Here, it is often seen as evidence that those in the middle of Roman society, like Thorstein Veblen's nineteenth-century American nouveau riche, "aped their social betters" in the hopes of earning respectability (as discussed in Chapter 3 regarding the Barberini Togatus). Thus the veristic style "trickled down" from patrician portraits sculpted in the round to two-dimensional depictions of the lower classes, inevitably declining in quality, taste, and specific meaning along the way (Kleiner 1977, 118–57; Wallace-Hadrill 1994, 143–74; Zanker 1999; Clarke 2003; for a critique, see Petersen 2006 and Mayer 2012). Another strand of the literature has emphasized the different connotations of the style depending on the patron: in images of butchers and craftsmen at Ostia, pride in their work (Kampen 1981); in portraits of freed *patres familias*, pride in their self-determination and authority within their household (Kockel 1993; Zanker 1995; Mayer 2012).

My observation about this literature is epistemological, not interpretive. All of it assumes that freedmen and middle-class craftsmen and businessmen commissioned veristic portraits of themselves exclusively in relief formats, and that those sculpted in the round were created for patricians. What is the evidence for this classification? How do we know that none of the now disembodied marble heads depicted freedmen? The answer seems to be simply that such works are deemed too high in quality to have been made for former slaves. John Pollini has recently articulated this view in stark terms:

> In seeking out the best Greek sculptors to translate their countenances into bronze and marble, the Roman nobility made Hellenistic visual culture their own. These new symbols of "Romanitas"—a high quality Romanized form of Hellenized portrait sculpture and the wax ancestral mask tradition that lay behind it—Roman freedmen sought to imitate in their own funerary portraiture. However, in the local workshops' mass-produced crude or less refined freedmen portraits, the visual language of the nobility was reduced to an imagery of utter banality. (Pollini 2007, 261)

According to this logic, portraits of nobles (high quality and Greek-made) and portraits of freedmen (crude, banal, and produced by local craftsman) can thus never be mistaken for one another. Like the opulent but tasteless decor of the fictional freedman Trimalchio, an artwork's base origins will always give themselves away. Whether you are a slave-turned-magnate or a soldier-turned-emperor, class will out.

In a striking case at the 2011 Portraiture exhibition at the Capitoline Museum, the prospect of freedmen patronage of a work of outstanding quality seems to have caused the show's organizers some unease. The object in question is the ungrounded, highly unusual double portrait of a couple, attached at the base up to the shoulder, now in the Vatican (Museo Pio Clementino, Sala dei Busti, inv. 592; Spinola 1999, 70n. 4) (Fig. 16). Volume XXX of the Barberini Codex, probably written in 1580, gives a detailed description of this work among the antiquities in the garden of Cardinal Alessandro Medici and records an inscription then still attached to it: *Gratidia M. l. / Chrite // M. Gratidius / Libanus* (Hülsen 1913; CIL vi, 35397). By 1613, ownership had passed to the Mattei family; it appears in a family inventory of that date as a portrait of Portia and Brutus "con un piedistallo tutto intagliato con littere" ("with a base all carved with letters") (Schröter 1993, 106 and 120n. 30). This puzzling notice would seem to indicate both that the

Figure 16 Double half-portraits in marble of Gratidia M. L. Chrite and M. Gratidius Libanus, probably originally a relief. Findspot unknown. First attested in 1580 in the collection of Alessandro Medici, according to the Barberini Codex XXX, 89. In the Maffei family inventory of 1613; sold to the Vatican Museum in 1770. Photo by Sergy Sosnovskiy.

inscribed base was still part of the work, and that the names it records were discounted in favor of the Matteis' own identification of the couple. It was perhaps shortly after this moment that the enframing marble block was cut away and the relief transformed into the unusual hybrid form we see today. Subsequent seventeenth- and eighteenth-century commentaries all either accept the romantic late Republican identification, or tweak it slightly (Cato and Portia, or Paetus and Arria), suggesting that the inscribed names were, by that point, gone and forgotten. The double portrait entered the Vatican collection in 1770, where it was (again?) heavily restored. Ennio Quirino Visconti, Helbig, and Amelung rejected all of the proposed names, praising the couple instead as anonymous but virtuous, hard-working members of the late Republican Roman bourgeoisie (Visconti 1807, 45–7; Helbig 1891, 143; Amelung 1908, 572–4). In 1913, Christian Hülsen made the connection between this work and the object described in the Barberini Codex, and recognized the lost inscription as proof of the couple's freedmen status (or, in the case of the husband, probably that of a freeborn son of a freedman). Zanker discussed the work in his 1975 study of freedmen funerary reliefs (Zanker 1975, 285–7). The freedmen identification is strongly supported not only by the inscription but also by the iconography of the *dextrarum iunctio*, as well as that of the half-bust format of an outward-facing couple, both closely comparable to the imagery of many freedmen funerary *a cassetta* reliefs (in which the figures appear to be looking out of a window). It has been understood in that milieu ever since (Kleiner 1977, 215n. 34; Pietrangeli 1982, 210–11n. 129; Volpi 1986–87, 270–1; Daltrop 1990, 192–3; Kockel 1993, 188–90; George 2005, 44).

However, this was challenged by the Portraiture exhibit at the Capitoline (La Rocca et al. 2011, 240). The lengthy entry in the catalog accepts the Gratidii identification. But, simultaneously, it takes the carving in the round to be ancient, i.e. not a product of reworking at the time of the removal of the inscribed frame. The text proposes that the original work consisted of attached busts set in a niche, not a typical freedmen relief *a cassetta*. The high quality of the portraits is taken as further evidence against the freedmen identification: "although often characterized by lively, expressive accents, those [freedmen] funerary reliefs usually display a rather more approximate and immediate sculptural style (*più approssimativo e immediato*), far from the formal quality" of this pair. A better comparison, we are told, is with "the best funerary portraits from the ancient capital," in particular the so-called Crassus portrait from the Tomb of the Licinii (the similarities have also been noted by Kockel 1993, 189). Stylistically, the affinities between the two works are indeed notable. Both Crassus and M. Gratidius Libanus are shown as square-jawed, hollow-cheeked men in their late fifties, with faint crows-feet and foreheads creased by long, evenly spaced horizontal lines. Both sculptors excelled at depicting the dynamic interplay between loose, hanging skin and the subcutaneous armature of bone and muscle. But what these similarities indicate, I would argue, is not that the Gratidii portraits must have belonged to something other than an *a cassetta* relief adorning the exterior of a freedman funerary monument (something more aristocratic, as per the Capitoline exhibit). Rather, they suggest that there was no intrinsic limit on the quality of artworks produced for freedmen patrons.

There are, in fact, some examples of high quality, marble portrait heads carved in the round that can be confidently identified as freedmen, such as the three superb portraits recovered in Columbarium II at Vigna Codini in 1847, or that of a young woman with an unusual hairstyle discovered at a columbarium on via Latina, near the Convent of Marianist Fathers, and now on display at the Palazzo Massimo (Anderson and Nista 1988, 76–81). Neither style nor quality would have identified the sitters as freedmen had these portraits surfaced on the art market. Their recovery in columbaria, a type of underground vault lined with niches that contained the cremated remains of members of a collective burial society (*collegia*), makes that identification very likely (on columbaria, see the forthcoming study by Dorian Borbonus). Could some of the hundreds of other empty niches at these sites, looted for centuries, or at any of the other columbaria around Rome (of which at least 16 are known), have furnished some portion of the 330 veristic portraits in Croz's catalog? Paul Zanker has recently suggested as much, citing the excellent state of preservation of many of the heads (Zanker 2011, 119n. 25). (Zanker leaves unexplored the likely implication of his suggestion, namely that they would have portrayed freedmen.) The hypothesis is unprovable, but it reminds us of the unconsidered possibilities and unasked questions, and exposes how tightly closed the hermeneutic circle of connoisseurship and social art history has been for this material.

One could argue that the high quality of the Vigna Codini portraits is an exception, since epigraphic evidence indicates that these particular slaves and ex-slaves had been employed in households of the extended imperial family. But there are no imperial connections behind the equally stunning and skillfully carved group of statues and herms dedicated by the freedman actor Caius Fundilius in a small room at the Sanctuary of Diana at Nemi. Jane Fejfer has recently offered a fascinating interpretation of the formal, iconographic, and epigraphic interrelationships among these sculptures; I note here only some of the evidence and her findings (Fejfer 2008, 285–305). The most important statue in the group is that of Fundilius, the dedicator (Fig. 17). He wears a toga and probably held a scroll in his hand; there is a scroll-bucket at his feet. Repeating inscriptions on the base and the bucket describe him as "doctus" (learned), and identify him as a member of a theatrical troupe called the Parasites of Apollo. Three of the inscribed herms found here also identify the sitters as members of this troupe, but Fundilius alone is singled out by the language and iconography of an educated man. Such aspirations may also explain the inclusion in the ensemble of a herm-portrait of a rhetor, Quintus Hostius Capito. Another herm depicts a local questor, whom Fejfer speculates may have had a business connection to the troupe. The only other full portrait-statue in the room honored Fundilia Rufa, Fundilius' *patrona*, who is portrayed with a bony, aged face and the extremely old-fashioned *tutulus* hairstyle (worn by Etruscan women, and discussed by Varro in his *De lingua Latina*, 7.44), as if she were an ancestor from the distant past. Fundilia is commemorated a second time by an unusual herm

Figure 17　Marble portrait statue of C. Fundilius Doctus, Ny Carlsberg Glyptotek, inv. I.N. 707. Found at the Sanctuary of Diana at Nemi, in the late nineteenth century, in the "Room of Fundilia" along with one other portrait statue, four complete herm portraits, as well as two additional heads and two herm shafts. Sold to the museum via Wolfgang Helbig.

with archaizing folds of drapery; this second portrait also wears the *tutulus*.

The ensemble is more than the sum of its parts. Roman authors expressed deep disdain for actors, but Fundilius does not hesitate to present himself as an elite, cultivated man: a proud, confident leader of an accomplished troupe, with prominent social connections and a distinguished ancestor. Little of this would have been discernible from any of these statues had they come down to us singly through the market, let alone from just the heads, which would scarcely have been identified as freedmen (Fejfer 2008, 4). Fejfer also emphasizes the diversity of the styling of the portraits, which had previously been taken as evidence of varying dates of manufacture (Moltesen 1997, 144). Their affiliation with a single dedication is confirmed not only by the social links among them but also by isotopic analysis, which indicates that five of the herms were carved from the same block of marble. They remind us once again that style necessarily corresponds neither to date nor to social class: "The best workshops could fulfill their client's desires to represent particular aspects of their identity or ancestry, or even give the statue an air of contemporaneity, luxury, or verism in accord (or in contrast) with current trends" (Fejfer 2008, 305). Of course, this complexity can only be appreciated when we know where and with what other works the object was displayed, or at the very least, when we have secure data (such as an inscription) about the patron's identity. In the absence of such information, it is difficult to avoid contextualizing works according to our own preconceived ideas, which sometimes reflect unexamined assumptions about the relationship between art and class.

When we write histories of Roman art based on ungrounded objects, the stories we tell are often populated by stock characters—reactionary aristocrats, vain women, striving middle classes, tasteless freedmen, bumbling provincials, thuggish soldiers. Such interpretations are justified, in a way, by these characters' appearances in ancient literature. The result might pass as social art history insofar as the artworks are being given not just a date but also a place within the larger cultural patterns of the Roman world. But as many scholars of classical literature have pointed out, when we rely uncritically upon literary texts for our understanding of the past, we adopt and affirm the elite, male worldview of the ancient authors (Pomeroy 1975; Foley 1981; Cameron and Kuhrt 1984; Habinek 1998; Dixon 2001). Students of ungrounded artworks can only interpret them *with* the grain of the literary sources, fitting them into pre-existing social models. Students of grounded objects can read them *against* the grain. Proud, successful, educated actor-freedmen like Fundilius, or competent, powerful priestess-benefactors like Perge's Aurelia Paulina (discussed in Chapter 2) are social types that do not exist in Roman literature; nor have they left us their own written accounts of how they perceived themselves and their relationship to society. We hear their voices only by paying close attention to the choices they made in their monuments—the pose, coiffure, age, costume, attributes, site, companions, inscriptions, and degree of assimilation to, or divergence from, established models and prototypes that they (or their flatterers) chose for their images. Careful formal analysis of grounded objects has the potential to tell us things about the Roman world that we cannot learn from texts.

Red Herrings

Unknown unknowns

"The most famous works of art are—and perhaps are destined to remain—the most mysterious. In fact, we hardly pay attention to their origins." With these words, Eugenio La Rocca, the Sovraintendente ai Beni Culturali of Rome, opened a day-long conference in 2008 on the Lupa Capitolina (quoted by Bartoloni 2010, 8). The symposium was occasioned by conservator Anna Maria Carruba's recent discovery that the bronze sculpture was cast as a single piece, not in smaller components that were then soldered together, as was much more common for bronze statuary in the ancient world. The renowned image of the She-wolf, part of the Capitoline collection since the fourteenth century (the twins are a later, Renaissance addition), has been reproduced on Italian postage stamps and on A. S. Roma paraphernalia, featured in the works of Lord Byron, Jackson Pollock, and Federico Fellini, and replicated in modern public monuments in over 20 countries (Mazzoni 2010). But Carruba concluded that this quintessential symbol of ancient Rome is in fact a work of the Middle Ages (Carruba 2006). In light of her findings (subsequently supported by thermoluminscence and radiocarbon tests: La Regina 2008; Martini 2010), the sculpture looks very different. Experts on ancient bronze-casting techniques have pointed out that the rough patina would be unique for an ancient work of this scale (Mazzeo 2005; Formigli 2010). Iconographic affinities with the thirteenth-century stone lions flanking the entrance to the Parma Duomo were noted (Carruba 2006, 40–2). Even those who continue to support the ancient date (and there are many) observed, for the first time, stylistic similarities with works from the Near East (Colonna 2010; La Rocca 2010).

The jury is still out on the date of the Lupa Capitolina (Warden 2011; most recently, Edilberto Formigli has argued that the work we see today is a medieval copy of an Etruscan original, produced by means of an imprint mold: Formigli 2012). What the episode has nevertheless revealed is how complacently the conventional wisdom on this canonical work had been passed down for generations—how little attention paid to its epistemological foundations or to the work's stylistic anomalies. It also suggests that neither an artwork's long tenure in a major collection nor its long-standing prominence in the historiography guarantee the correctness of our connoisseurial attributions. In the case of (ostensibly) ancient works, we could be off by decades, centuries, or even millennia.

This point is important for thinking about the great bogeyman that lurks around all discourses (commercial and scholarly) involving ungrounded ancient art: forgery. A cherished axiom of connoisseurship, set down by Friedländer, is that in the long run, the eye of the connoisseur always trumps the hand of the forger (e.g. Spencer 2004a, 74; Sutton 2007, 16). Friedländer argued that fakes reflect the tastes and aesthetics of their moment of creation, embedded in them like DNA, and that once contemporary tastes move on, forgeries are left standing in the dust, their modernity naked and exposed (Friedländer 1960 [1942], 258–66). Indeed, it is hard to believe that Hans van Meegeren's 1930s "Vermeers," with their heavy-lidded, Marlene Dietrich-esque Christs, would have stood the test of time, even if Van Meegeren hadn't been forced to confess. "Forgeries must be served hot, as they come out of the oven" (Friedländer 1960 [1942], 261).

The notion that forgeries have a short shelf-life is reassuring, but how can we possibly know if it is correct? In a public lecture about fakes, Theodore Rousseau, former curator of European art at the Metropolitan Museum, is said to have admitted frankly at the start that, "We should all realize that we can only talk about the bad forgeries, the ones that have been detected; the good ones are still hanging on the walls" (Lynes 1968, 21; see also Jones 1990, 332, on "the limits of expertise"; Lenain 2011, 271 and passim). Friedländer never acknowledged the possibility of undetected fakes. Does the fact that multiple generations of scholars have looked at an artwork carefully without questioning its attribution prove that the attribution is correct, or does it prove the conservative, tradition-bound nature of scholarly disciplines? In the Roman field, the problem is particularly acute, since so many of the canonical works are both exceptional, even unique (e.g. the Barberini Togatus, the Fonseca bust, the Capitoline Brutus, the Trebonianus Gallus statue), *and* lacking in reliable external evidence regarding their date. Ironically, the position of these ungrounded works at the very heart of the discipline has shielded them from the meticulous and skeptical scrutiny they would doubtless attract if they were to surface on the market today. It is, for example, a simple and readily observable fact that the tall crown of long, loose ringlets worn over the brow of the Fonseca figure is more typical of the hairstyles at the court of Louis XIV than those of ancient Rome, where it is attested in no grounded works and in only a very small handful of ungrounded ones. That this has been pointed out so rarely (only once, to my knowledge: Mannsperger 1998, 70) indicates, if nothing else, how much faith we put in the opinions of our disciplinary forebears.

It is, of course, through a close analysis of the forms and style of the Fonseca bust that I perceive anomalies (her hairstyle, coquettish pose, and carving techniques). An attribution based on this evidence to, say, the early eighteenth century would be connoisseurship, and would have no more and no less epistemological validity than other connoisseurial attributions. I aim not, in other words, to convince my reader that the piece is a forgery, but rather to remind him or her of how much we simply *do not know* about this sculpture, contrary to what one might assume from its near ubiquity in the historiography. The case is, in this regard, similar to that of the Lupa. Due to our faith in connoisseurship to supply the fundamental historical data, and to the conservative nature of scholarly traditions, we have effectively forgotten how many uncertainties encumber the ungrounded, canonical works of Roman art. They have become, to borrow Donald Rumsfeld's phrase, unknown unknowns.

The matter of forgery is, arguably, only a small piece of this larger predicament and a distracting one. In much of the literature, both scholarly and popular, it is presented as a very bad thing. Thierry Lenain has recently traced this "rhetoric of execration" to Paul Eudel's admonitory collector's handbook of 1884, *Le truquage: altérations, fraudes, contrefaçons dévoilées* (Lenain 2011, 252–4). Eudel described forgers as termites, undermining the art world "in darkness and silence." They are criminals who "must not be spared," their works "parasitic vegetation." Friedländer likened fakes to hybrid monsters, neither fully of one period nor the other (Friedländer 1960 [1942], 237). Karl Meyer compared forgeries to venereal disease, "the punishment for excessive desire and bad judgment" (Meyer 1973, 108). Robert Steven Bianchi called fakes a pollution, citing examples where good works were rejected because they did not conform to the standard set by fakes (Bianchi 2000, 12–13).

A common trope in the literature is forgery as crime-scene, casting the connoisseur who reads the clues and discovers the truth as genius detective (Ginzburg 1980; Elsner 1990; Shanks 1996, 37–41). One of the first police officials to head a unit specializing in art forgery, Guy Isnard, working in Paris in the 1950s, wrote a memoire called *True or False? The Investigations of the Sherlock Holmes of Painting*. Picking up on this image, the dust jacket of former Metropolitan Museum Director Thomas Hoving's self-aggrandizing book on "fake-busting" features campy photographs of Hoving in a fedora looking through a large magnifying glass (Hoving 1996). In Robertson Davies' 1985 novel, *What's Bred in the Bone*, the protagonist's ingenious identification of a South American monkey in a painting allegedly by van Eyck dramatically exposes the forgery, vanquishing Nazis in the process. These ominous metaphors—termites, monsters, venereal disease, crimes, Nazis—are reassuring, in that they construe forgeries as freakish aberrations from an otherwise healthy, safe, stable field. They suggest that good "fake-busters" can solve the crime, apprehend

the bad guy, remove the pollution, and restore order and epistemological certainty to the land.

Alas, the problem is more complicated, at least in Roman art
history. Purging forgeries will not purify the corpus, because the
source of its instability is not a handful of fakes but a profusion of
ungrounded works. These can only be situated somewhere along a
long grey scale of greater or lesser consensus about their antiquity. At
one end are the majority, works such as the Capitoline bust of Cicero
or the Bevilacqua portrait of Augustus wearing a laurel wreath, which
have never, to my knowledge, been publicly doubted. At the other
end are Charles Townley's head of Nero and his beloved "Clytie" at
the British Museum, once believed in, but now widely (perhaps even
universally) condemned. At various points in between these two poles
are the objects that have been questioned, quietly or noisily, such as
the Warren Cup in the British Museum, the Arricia head of Augustus
in Boston, the Cleveland Jonah statuettes, the green schist portrait of
Julius Caesar in Berlin, and the Marius and Sulla portraits in Munich.

This grey scale is rarely acknowledged. The authenticity of
ungrounded objects—especially the long-famous ones—is usually
taken for granted. The whole question of forgery has an air of the
distasteful about it; suspicions are more often whispered than published
(Muscarella 2000, 3, attributes this to fear of reprisals). No wonder,
given the widespread perception of fakes as shocking, horrific, exceptional things like venereal diseases or murders, rather than simply
as one end of the spectrum that Roman art historians engage with
whenever they write about ungrounded objects.

"From Egypt, exact provenance unknown"

A recent museum exhibition on forgery illustrates the ways in which
discussions of the phenomenon can miss its larger methodological
and theoretical implications. Held at the Brooklyn Museum in 2009,
"Unearthing the Truth: Egypt's Pagan and Coptic Sculpture" featured

31 objects from the museum's permanent collection (Russmann 2009). Ten of these, all acquired between the 1950s and 1970s, when the booming demand for "Coptic" material far exceeded the supply, are now deemed by the museum to be fakes. The show was laudable for its frank treatment of this material and for avoiding the shameful rhetoric of pollution, sin, or murder in its discussion of these fascinating works. But despite such an exhibit's ostensibly self-reflexive nature (e.g. Jones 1990), this one refused to pull back the curtain to explain why mistakes have been made in the past, how they were discovered, or to acknowledge that they could be made again.

Instead, the stance adopted was one of infallible connoisseurship by authority. The claim to black-and-white certainty manifested itself very literally in the exhibition space. The authentic pieces were displayed in masterpiece theater-style (see Chapter 2), floating in glowing, spotlit cases in a darkened gallery. The fakes, by contrast, were shown in a flatly illuminated white room at the end. Among the forgeries, some assessable data was presented. The catalog helpfully explains that some pieces have been condemned because they are carved in a type of heavily pitted, nummilitic limestone not used in antiquity (nos. 30 and 31), or because they show suspicious patterns of damage (restricted to bodily extremities or backgrounds, while faces are well-preserved) (nos. 22, 23, 24, and 29). In other cases, however, while the research behind the scenes was no doubt more nuanced, the only fault discussed is the poor quality of the carving (a lion on no. 26 is "earless and comically ill-drawn") or the apparently "ridiculous" iconography (no. 27, which features snakes whose coils "defy logic" and whose ends morph into bird heads and plants). To the inexpert observer, however, it is hard to see what makes this carving or this iconography so much more problematic than that of the images in the "good" half, where one finds just as many implausible creatures and sketchily rendered bodies (but here described not as comical or ridiculous but rather as "rendered with great naïveté"; no. 2). The authenticity of the objects in the first half of the show (acquired through the same or different channels as the fakes? The catalog doesn't say) is presumed rather than demonstrated. The subjectivity of the judgments—or possibility for error—is never acknowledged. The confident positivism, already evident in the exhibit's title, was bait for at least one reviewer, who voiced doubts about seven of the 21 "good" pieces (Kruglov 2010).

Also problematic was the way "Unearthing the Truth" treated the matter of findspot. It is unclear what role, if any, archaeological data played in the judgments, or indeed, whether the ostensibly authentic pieces are grounded or ungrounded. The provenance information was inconsistent and often ambiguous. Eight of the labels stated unequivocally that the object is from a particular site, but no specific discussion of or bibliography on the alleged discovery was provided. Other works in this half of the show were "said to be" or "possibly" from a particular site. The most common label in the exhibit, appearing on nine of the 21 apparently authentic works, confounds: "from Egypt, exact provenance unknown." What does this mean? "Egypt" is indeed a rather inexact findspot. If nothing else, the phrase implies that the curator has harder data about the origins of these nine objects than she does about, say, the four in the forgery section labeled "provenance unknown." Is this so? Or was the ambiguous phrase meant to blunt the fact that the pieces deemed "good" are as ungrounded (and thus, arguably, as uncertain) as the fakes? Either way, in an exhibition whose stated goal is to "raise awareness" of the issues of forgery (Russmann 2009, 18), this confusing label, like the show's general lack of critical reflexivity, is counterproductive.

Licit/illicit

Concerns about forgery obscure the deeper epistemological problems inherent in ungrounded antiquities. Also distracting is the question of whether antiquities are "licit" or "illicit" (e.g. Brodie and Tubb 2002; Renfrew 2010). This language is used chiefly by those seeking to draw attention to the problem of looting and to the prohibitions against the exportation of cultural property that most nations have passed (e.g. Renfrew 2000; Brodie et al. 2006; Waxman 2008a; Felch and Frammolino 2011; Dyson 2012). Signatories to the 1970 UNESCO Convention on the Means of Prohibiting and Preventing the Illicit Import, Export and Transfer of Ownership of Cultural Property have agreed to respect those laws (Vrdoljak 2006). The principle was tested in U.S. courts in 2002, when Frederick Schultz, the head of the National Association of Dealers in Ancient, Oriental and Primitive Art, was convicted of handling goods whose exportation violated Egypt's patrimony laws (Gerstenblith 2003 and 2006). Soon thereafter began the wave of repatriations to Italy of artworks that had passed through the hands of convicted trafficker Giacomo Medici, and the Italian trial of former Getty curator Marion True (Watson and Todeschini 2006; Felch and Frammolino 2011). These cases have raised public awareness of the UNESCO accord and of the relationship between the art market and looting (e.g. Eakin 2006; Kimmelman 2006; Kennedy and Eakin 2006; Lacayo 2008; Murr 2008; Gopnik 2012). The Convention and its date have, as a result, become the touchstone in almost all public discourse surrounding ungrounded antiquities. Many policies have been shaped around it, some going back decades, such as the publication policy of the *American Journal of Archaeology* (noted in Chapter 3) (Kleiner 1990; Kyrieleis 2000; Norman 2005). Others are more recent, such as the 2008 acquisitions guidelines of the Association of Art Museum Directors, which urges members not to acquire a piece "unless research substantiates that the work was outside its country of probable modern discovery before 1970 or was legally exported from its probable country of modern discovery after 1970." Broadly speaking, antiquities without documentary proof of exportation prior to 1970 are seen as "illicit" (if not quite outright illegal), as they could be subject to a repatriation claim, whereas antiquities with such a paper trail are "licit," as they are unlikely to be subject to such claims (although Egypt and Turkey have recently stepped up demands for objects removed a century ago).

The widening attention and adherence to the terms of the 1970 UNESCO accord have had salutary effects. Since 2006, when the

repatriation stories became big news, market prices of licit antiquities have been steadily rising over illicit ones (Elia 2009b; Silver
2009, 298; Melikian 2012). It can be hoped that this will decrease the
incentives for looting. For those in the business of studying the past
rather than buying and selling it, however, all ungrounded antiquities
are problematic, whether they surfaced in 1974 or 1749. The much-
underscored distinction between licit antiquities and illicit ones is a
red herring.

Consider, for example, the debate surrounding the publication of
recently surfaced, undocumented antiquities. The *American Journal of
Archaeology* "will not serve for the announcement or initial scholarly
presentation of any object in a private or public collection acquired
after December 30, 1973 [when the policy was formulated], unless its
existence is documented before that date, or it was legally exported
from the country of origin." In 1990, Fred Kleiner, the editor of the
journal, clarified the policy and its aims:

> By taking such a position, the AIA is saying that it will not assist
> those acquiring antiquities without pedigree or export permit to
> enhance the market value or perceived importance of their acquisi-
> tions by presenting them for the first time under the aegis of (and
> with the implied stamp of approval of) the Archaeological Institute of
> America. In this way the AIA is expressing its opposition to the illicit
> export of antiquities and the despoliation of archaeological sites that is
> often caused by the search for statues, vases, jewelry, coins and other
> objects of proven commercial value. The acquisition of antiquities
> by illicit means almost always also results in the irretrievable loss to
> scholarship of all information regarding the provenience and context
> of those artifacts, information that is vital for a full understanding of
> the pieces in question. (Kleiner 1990)

Comparable policies have been adopted by several other scholarly
organizations, including the American School of Oriental Research,
the College Art Association, and the German Archaeological Institute
(e.g. Kyrieleis 2000). These policies have been controversial. Some have
argued that they amount to censorship and only compound the loss

of historical knowledge occasioned by the objects' looting in the first place (e.g. Muscarella 1984; Boardman 2006; Owen 2009). The policy was revised slightly in 2004 to allow for the publication of "unprovenanced" (i.e. ungrounded) pieces if the fact of their lack of history was integral to the discussion. Editor Naomi Norman explained:

> The intent here is to keep the checkered past of an object out in the open and part of the continuing scholarly discussion of that piece. All too often, once a piece gets "proper scholarly presentation" and the debate begins, scholars forget that the object is without archaeological context and may have come to the market illegally ... The intent of this revision is to try to keep the spotlight on the problem [of the illicit trade in antiquities], even after an illicit object has become part of standard scholarship. The point is to remind us all of how much information and value is lost when an object is illegally removed from its archaeological context. (Norman 2005)

Norman seeks to encourage discussion of missing archaeological contexts. But the policy still concerns only ungrounded objects that surfaced after 1973. Her worries, however, are even more germane to the ungrounded artworks that have been part of the field for decades or centuries than they are to recently surfaced ones, which most scholars know to handle with caution. For example, in the mid-nineteenth century, the Metropolitan Museum's Trebonianus Gallus statue belonged to a French architect, Auguste de Montferrand, employed at the court in St. Petersburg. The 1852 catalog of his collection claimed that the bronze had been discovered during an early nineteenth-century excavation near the Lateran in Rome, undertaken by a Russian count, who had found the work beside a pedestal in a large hall (von Köhne 1852, 3). There are no other records or notices of this alleged excavation. The early curators at the Metropolitan mistrusted the story. In her catalog of the Greek and Roman bronzes, Gisela Richter noted that "the circumstances told of [the statue's] discovery are somewhat suspicious, and it is doubtful whether the story is based on any facts" (Richter 1915, 156). With the passage of time, however, her well-founded skepticism was forgotten. The alleged findspot is ignored all together in six subsequent scholarly publications of the statue; it is given with the "said to be" formula in three; and it is repeated (wholly or in part), with no indication that it is anything less than a secure fact, in nine (Marlowe forthcoming). To some, it confirmed the identification of the statue as a soldier-emperor: "This statue of the soldier-emperor would have been a fitting climax for the hall, perhaps of a military camp [the headquarters of the *equites singulares*], where it was found near St. John in the Lateran in Rome" (McCann 1981, 632). Rumors sometimes congeal into "facts," atop which historical interpretations are built, their shaky foundations hidden.

It is precisely the long-famous pieces like the Trebonianus statue, the Fonseca bust, or the Barberini Togatus whose epistemology is in greatest need of critical re-examination, whose "lack of history" should be an "integral" part of any discussion of them. Their canonical status has lulled us into a false sense of security; few scholars are cognizant of how murky many such works' origins actually are. The problems posed by ungrounded antiquities might be more fully addressed by publication policies that required a full, explicit account of the origins and ownership history of every piece discussed, regardless of when it surfaced and whether or not it is "licit."

Repatriation and recontextualization

The epistemological hazards posed by ungrounded objects have been eclipsed by the legal concerns surrounding those exported after 1970. Also symptomatic of these perhaps somewhat misplaced priorities is some of the rhetoric around the repatriation of looted antiquities. There are many reasons to support repatriation claims beyond the hope that they will depress the market and thereby decrease the incentives for looting. One could argue that repatriation rights various social and historical wrongs (Barkan 2002), and that it earns goodwill in countries where one might wish to excavate or whose artworks one might like to borrow for temporary exhibits (Bauer et al. 2007). More tenuous, but nonetheless frequently asserted, is the notion that the return of looted antiquities can somehow restore lost archaeological context. In this section, I will discuss four case studies where this claim was made, and consider some of the obstacles to its realization.

Nostoi

A subtext of the first public exhibition of artworks returned to Italy as a result of Giacomo Medici's conviction was that repatriation entails recontextualization. Held in 2007–8 at the Quirinal Palace in Rome, the show was titled "Nostoi," the Greek word for "homecomings," and also the term used to characterize a whole group of ancient tales—of which Homer's *Odyssey* is the best known—about the returns of the Greek heroes after the Trojan War. The name implied that, like Odysseus reuniting with his wife and child after years of trial and trauma, these stolen works were at last returning to their true, original homes (Godart and de Caro 2007, 14–20). In his catalog essay, Louis Godart, "Consigliere" for the Preservation of Italian Artistic Patrimony, claims that:

> To fully appreciate a masterpiece, one must connect it to the world that saw its creation. The efforts of all—archaeologists, researchers, museum directors—must thus aim to reconstruct around every work of art the context in which it was created and in which it was subsequently deposited. (Godart and de Caro 2007, xx)

These masterpieces couldn't be fully appreciated in Boston or Malibu, Godart implies, because that was not the "context" of their manufacture or deposition. Relocating them to the Quirinal Palace is the first step in the process of "reconstructing" that context.

This reassuring message was reinforced by the show's lone foreign venue, the new Acropolis Museum in Athens—a remarkable choice, given that the museum was still under construction at the time and had not yet officially opened to the public. The top floor of the new Acropolis Museum was to house the architectural sculptures from the Parthenon—all but those despoiled by Lord Elgin for now, but eventually, it was hoped, those too. The layout of that gallery would echo that of the temple and offer floor-to-ceiling window views out to the real thing. As the architectural competition and extensive media coverage had made clear, the design was intended as a declaration not only of Greece's ability to care for the sculptures, but also of the superiority of this housing to any other, since here alone the sculptures would be as close to recontextualized—reintegrated into their original setting—as they possibly could be in any museum.

The choice of "Nostoi" as the inaugural exhibit at the new Acropolis Museum was doubtless a way for Greece to yoke this important precedent for the return of plundered artworks to its own cause. Conversely, Italian cultural officials may have hoped that some of the international passion and moral righteousness surrounding the Elgin Marbles case would rub off on their own, much more strictly legally based repatriation claims. They may also have believed that the exhibition of the "Nostoi" objects in this particular museum would bolster their assertion that repatriation entails recontextual-ization. In fact, the juxtaposition of the two cases—the Parthenon sculptures and the "Nostoi" artworks—ultimately underscores their profound differences in this regard. In the case of the former, we can pinpoint their precise original positions on the ancient temple, and install and interpret them accordingly. Of the latter, by contrast, we know far less—sometimes the name of a particular site (e.g. Cerveteri), sometimes as little as a broad region (e.g. Campania). Rarely can the Medici archive shed light on what type of sites those findspots were (tombs, houses, temples, etc.), or what other objects were found there. Our enduring ignorance of the "Nostoi" objects' ancient settings is clear from their exhibition labels, which say little beyond "formerly in the collection of the Getty Museum" or some other American institution. Despite their repatriation, the "Nostoi" artworks stubbornly resist recontextualization.

Ascoli Satriano marbles

In addition to source countries seeking the return of their cultural patrimony, archaeologists themselves sometimes suggest that recontextualization can result from repatriation. Colin Renfrew has written optimistically about "post-disjunctive forensic recontextualization," "the possibility, after a catastrophic episode of looting, to use investigative techniques to bring about the restoration of aspects of the original context of discovery" (Renfrew 2010). The example he cites is an extraordinary group of painted marble tomb-sculptures (Bottini and Setari 2009). Two of the pieces had been acquired by the Getty Museum in 1985, but their common origin was not known or acknowledged by the museum (at least not publicly; Silver 2009, 65–7). Viewed in isolation, one of them, with its stunningly well-preserved pigments and theatrical depiction of a pair of griffins devouring a fallen doe, was so unusual that Renfrew, as he admits, had assumed it was a forgery. Then in 2006, in response to the extensive press about looting, patrimony, and American museums, an Italian man living near Ascoli Satriano in Apulia came forward and claimed to have been part of a group of *tombaroli* that had found several sculptures in 1976 or 1977. Most, he said, had been seized by the Guardia di Finanza of Foggia in 1978, but a few, unbeknownst to the authorities, had already been sold by then. One of these, a group depicting griffins attacking a deer, was now, he had heard, in an American collection. The seized objects and police file from 1978 were tracked down. With help from evidence in the Medici archive, the details of the looting of this highly unusual ensemble of 11 painted marble sculptures emerged. According to Renfrew, we see, as a result, "not just a single, perhaps rather anomalous artwork, but a whole remarkable assemblage of objects: a partial reconstruction of one of the most remarkable tomb groups recovered from Magna Graecia, safely assigned to the fourth century BC and to Ascoli Satriano" (Renfrew 2010).

This is a happy outcome indeed. But it should be stressed that without the repentant *tombarolo*, this post-disjunctive recontextualization would not have happened. Even if, on the strength of the Medici documents, the Getty had returned its two pieces in 2005, the forensic evidence alone would not have reconnected the dots between them and the nine others sequestered in Foggia. An astute observer might have noticed stylistic similarities between the two groups of sculptures, but their association with one another would have remained speculative. The archives seized from the likes of Giacomo Medici, Robin Symes, and Gianfranco Becchina have much to tell us about the buying, selling, and smuggling of antiquities; and they make it easier to punish the middlemen and collectors, the so-called "real looters" (Elia 1993, 69; Renfrew 1993, 16). But with few exceptions, the files of these internationally-connected dealers don't take us all the way back to the place in the ground where an object was found, or to the other pieces that were part of the ancient ensemble (especially if the other pieces weren't marketable). For that, we need the real "real looters," the *tombaroli*, like the one who came forward in Ascoli Satriano. And even in this case, we still don't know exactly where the objects were found, and what kind of site it was (a recent article hypothesizes that it may have been a wealthy residence rather than a tomb, as is usually assumed; Gasparri and Guzzo 2005). Renfrew is sanguine, but I see this case as further proof that despite the best efforts of the courts and Interpol and U.S. Customs and the Comando Carabinieri per la Tutela del Patrimonio Culturale, we are doomed to remain in the dark about the ancient context of nearly all the ungrounded antiquities in our midst, repatriated or not.

Euphronios' Sarpedons

Like Colin Renfrew, Malcolm Bell, an archaeologist at the University of Virginia, has expressed hope that repatriation can enrich our historical understanding of a looted ancient artwork. Responding to Metropolitan Museum director Philippe de Montebello's doubts about such prospects for the Euphronios krater (which he'd just agreed to return to Italy), Bell wondered:

Was it [found in] one of the remarkable chamber tombs at Cerveteri, almost house-like in their complexity? What other objects were found inside? What individual did the krater accompany into the underworld? Who was its last owner, before it was acquired by the museum? What is the date of the burial? Could the tragic scene of Sarpedon's death have been chosen because Euphronios knew the vase would have a funerary use? Mr. de Montebello appears to be quite uninterested in such questions, but I believe that most viewers of the vase would like to know about the full history of its use in antiquity. *Once it is back in Italy perhaps at least some of this information can be recovered.* (Archaeological Institute of America 2006, emphasis added)

Sadly, this has not been the case. No new information about the vase's findspot has emerged as a result of its installation in a beautiful, ground-floor display at the Villa Giulia in Rome. The lack of firm data is particularly frustrating, because the famous krater is, amazingly, one of *two* Greek pots that surfaced in the 1970s signed by Euphronios and depicting the removal of Sarpedon's slain body (Silver 2009). The second is a kylix cup, with the scene painted below the rim on one its outer faces. Dealer Robert Hecht acquired both vessels from Giacomo Medici; a note in Hecht's memoir manuscript, seized in his Paris apartment in 2001, stated that they were found in the same tomb (Watson and Todeschini 2006, 160–79). He sold the krater to the Metropolitan in 1972, and failed to sell the kylix to that museum— still reeling from the outcry over the krater—the following year. It eventually went to Texas oilman Bunker Hunt in 1979. The painting on the kylix lacks the grace and balance of the famous krater: the composition is ungainly, its depiction of human anatomy awkward and fussy. Comparing the two works in a public lecture, Metropolitan Museum curator Dietrich von Bothmer argued that:

The cup … is an early work by Euphronios, if not his earliest. The Sarpedon krater shows him at the height of his mastery. The difference between the two vases, however, is more than mere technical competence. In the very treatment of the subject we see an inner progression

from a hesitant composition to a perfect solution. (von Bothmer 1981,
quoted in Silver 2009, 125–6)

When the Hunt collection was auctioned in 1990, the piece was bought
by Giacomo Medici, who was presumably hoping to flip it and reap
some of the staggering Euphronios bounty that had so far eluded him.
It was not to be. Italian authorities raided Medici's Geneva warehouse
in 1995; the kylix was among the hundreds of artworks they seized. It
is today housed at the Villa Giulia, where it has featured in a series of
rotating, one-room displays about looted antiquities. Its alleged ancient
tomb-mate, the krater formerly belonging to the Metropolitan, resides
one floor below. One hopes that the galleries will be reinstalled some
day and the two Euphronios Sarpedon vessels displayed side by side.
If that happens, art lovers will be able to compare and contrast the two
treatments of the subject, and ponder Euphronios' remarkable range or
trajectory, just as von Bothmer did in his slide lecture. It will be a form
of post-disjunctive recontextualization.

But how much more significant would this recontextualization
be if we could be certain that the story of the vessels' discovery in
the same Etruscan tomb were true! The historical import of the pair
would go far beyond the career of Euphronios. For the past 20 years,
the reception of Greek painted pottery in the ancient world has been a
focus of scholarly debate (ballast, cheap imitations of precious metal, or
high art?) (Vickers and Gill 1994; Shanks 1996, 37–41; Whitley 1997;
Oakley 1998; Reusser 2002). One family's ownership of two versions of
the same subject by the same artist in two very different styles would
constitute rare evidence that Etruscan consumers might have cared
about some of the same aesthetic aspects of Greek pottery that we
care about. The findspot information would take us, in other words,
from the realm of the artist to that of the user, from connoisseurship
to social art history. But despite their return to Italy, there is still no
more information about the vessels' discovery beyond the unsub-
stantiated, tantalizing rumor recorded in Hecht's memoir (which, to
complicate matters further, he subsequently claimed was pure fiction).

The repatriation of these looted artworks has not brought us any closer to their historical recontextualization.

Weary Herakles

As some of the previous cases suggest, recontextualization depends at least in part on *how* repatriated objects are displayed in their new setting. Sometimes, the installation thematizes the repatriation itself, at the expense of the object's ancient context. The display of the recently reunited halves of the Weary Herakles at the Antalya Museum in southern Turkey is one example of this. The justice of the return of the figure's upper portion by the Boston Museum of Fine Arts is beyond question. The evidence of its fit onto the lower half of the statue excavated at Perge is incontrovertible, even though it took almost 20 years for the American museum to accept this as proof of looting and to send its half back (Edgers 2011a). Happily, the statue has now been made whole again.

An even fuller "post-disjunctive recontextualization" for the Weary Herakles at the Antalya Museum, however, remains frustratingly unrealized. The statue was but one element of a spectacular sculpture dedication in a long hall at the South Bath complex at Perge, eight other components of which are also on display at the Antalya Museum. These include life-size statues of Aphrodite, Nemesis, Hygeia, Meleager, Apollo, and Marsyas, as well as the lovely "Dancing Girl" in grey and white marbles, which was, prior to the reintegration of the Herakles statue, the most famous piece in the museum. The local notable who donated the group in antiquity, Claudius Peison, went to great lengths to ensure that it be seen as a coherent whole, and that the whole ensemble be credited to him, by inscribing his name on the base of each of the statues (or, in the case of the Aphrodite, on the shield she holds). This makes it all the more disappointing that the nine sculptures are today scattered across four different galleries of the museum, their locations determined not by their findspot but by their subject matter. As we saw in Chapter 2, this is not the only ancient ensemble that was disaggregated upon arrival at the Antalya Museum, its constituent parts divvied up among separate galleries devoted to images of emperors, gods, heroes, or mortals. The one exception to this rule is the large hall dedicated to the Perge theater sculptures, installed in 1999. Statues and reliefs produced over the course of several centuries, depicting gods, emperors, heroes and private citizens, intermingle in the museum much as they did at the site, effectively evoking the riotous, visual field of an ancient theater façade.

The reunification of Claudius Peison's dedication would encourage viewers to see the statues not as solitary, timeless masterpieces but as components of a historically-specific ensemble, components which derived their meaning in relation to one another, to their particular site, and to the euergetistic ideology of their donor. Instead, in an extreme version of "masterpiece theater," the reintegrated Herakles statue is presented as a trophy, enshrined in isolation in a spotlit, red-velvet-draped vitrine, the climactic culmination of the museum's longest architectural vista. The other statues from Claudius Peison's dedication are nowhere in sight. A looped slideshow on video monitors flanking the vitrine mentions the statue's findspot and ancient patron only fleetingly. Instead, the slideshow focuses on the David-and-Goliath narrative of the "Homecoming of the Herakles" (brave Turkish archaeologist challenges rich, powerful foreign institution and eventually wins), told through newspaper clippings and conservation photographs.

The rare occasions when a repatriated object can rejoin the ensemble to which we know it belonged in antiquity are moments to rejoice. The public will better understand the tragedy of looting if museums and educators teach them how ancient artworks were shaped by their context. With its installation of the restored Weary Herakles, the Antalya Museum missed an opportunity to do so. Repatriation, especially when considered through the framework of the 1970 UNESCO convention, can be a distraction from the historical questions surrounding looted ancient artworks. Similarly, as I argued at the beginning of this chapter, a narrow focus on the risk of forgery

can obscure how much else we don't know about ungrounded antiquities. These two issues, repatriation and forgery, are red herrings,
drawing our attention away from the deeper epistemological matters
that should be of primary concern to whose who seek to learn about
the past from its material remains.

Conclusion: Best Practices

A ripe moment

It seems likely that the ongoing looting and repatriation controversy will result in an increased understanding of the history of ancient art history, how collections were formed, and for what larger ends. With the tightening of restrictions on the market, many classical curators have already begun to shift their attentions from the pursuit of new acquisitions to researching the archaeological and ownership histories of pieces in their collections (Cooke 2011). As a 2008 op-ed piece in the *New York Times* suggests, the public has come to expect greater transparency about such matters, due to increasing awareness not only of archaeological looting but of Nazi plunder as well (Waxman 2008b). Under Director Maxwell Anderson's leadership, the Dallas Museum of Art has become a model of candor and accountability in its handling of repatriation cases. In a highly visible section of the museum's website ("Deaccessions"), a detailed report on each case is presented, including "purchase information," "provenance supplied," "criteria for deaccessioning", and "evidence" (Dallas Museum of Art n.d.). One hopes that such full disclosure will become standard practice in the museum world, and for all objects in a given collection, not just those being returned. The Boston Museum of Fine Arts has also taken a lead in this regard. The webpage for each object in the ancient collection includes an ample section on "provenance," which presents all the available findspot information (including verified and unverified reports) as well as detailed ownership history. The Boston Museum was also the first, in 2010, to establish an endowed position for a Curator of Provenance (Edgers 2011b). The Getty Museum is following Boston's lead in these areas.

The role of the internet and digital technologies in smoothing the way for these changes is worth underscoring. Full disclosure of an object's ownership history can mean revealing dealers' names and even prices paid, and possibly also acknowledging one's own improper decisions, as the museums in Boston and Dallas have, respectively, done. Museum websites allow these potentially unsettling facts to be made public without forcing museumgoers to confront them in the space of the gallery itself. Indeed, websites and mobile apps can provide access to all sorts of information without cluttering museum walls and labels with distracting verbiage. The Cleveland Museum of Art has been experimenting quite successfully with rentable ipads, while the object pages of the Metropolitan Museum of Art's website offer rich discussions and links to related objects in the collection (for example, from the Caracalla head discussed in Chapter 2 to the two other fragments from the same statue displayed elsewhere in the museum).

The internet is also an especially effective medium for the publication of large databases. Various projects currently in the works suggest the some of the ways it can enrich our knowledge of ancient artworks. Jason Felch and Ralph Frammolino, reporters at the *Los Angeles Times* and authors of *Chasing Aphrodite: The Hunt for Looted Antiquities at the World's Richest Museum* (2011), have recently proposed a crowd-sourcing project called Wikiloot (http://chasingaphrodite.com/wikiloot). It would make available online the tens of thousands of photographs seized from Giacomo Medici and other convicted antiquities traffickers, allowing the public to spot (and report) matches between the still-dirt-encrusted objects in the snapshots and the spiffed up artworks now on pedestals in their local museums (or on their rich uncle's mantelpiece). Less legally and ethically complicated is Arachne, the enormous online photographic database of the German Archaeological Institute, undertaken by that organization in conjunction with the University of Cologne (http://arachne.uni-koeln.de). Another exciting new project under way is called Ubi Erat Lupa, based at the University of Salzburg (http://ubi-erat-lupa.org). Its aim is to create a massive photographic catalog of stone monuments (sculptures, reliefs, inscriptions, and architectural pieces) from prehistory to 500 CE. The current focus is on southeastern Europe, but the project has the capacity for "expansion in all geographic directions." These databases have the potential to bring to wider attention the thousands of largely unknown (but often richly grounded) works of ancient art currently languishing in small regional museums across the expanse of the former Roman Empire. This will make it easier for Roman art historians to incorporate such objects into their research and teaching, in place of the old standbys.

Digital technologies, new internet databases and shifting attitudes in the wake of the looting scandal have the potential to change the landscape of ancient art history. The moment is right to think critically about some of the discipline's long-standing methodologies and assumptions. Two broad commitments would, I believe, benefit the field: the prioritization of archaeological context and the full articulation of findspot, ownership, and comparative data for all objects discussed.

Prioritize archaeological context

The most fully contextualized objects deserve pride of place in our scholarship, exhibitions, and classrooms. The more we know about the findspot of a work of Roman art, the deeper we can understand its particular ancient history and significance, and the less we have to rely on preconceived ideas and generalizations to fill in the gaps. A session on Roman provincial art at the 2013 meeting of the College Art Association, chaired by Jim Frakes and Kimberly Cassibry, showcased rich, nuanced interpretations generated by the fertile combination of grounded objects and meticulous formal analysis. These included a portrait of Vibia Sabina from the theater at Sessa Aurunca, whose billowing drapery perhaps likened her to "Aura," and thus flattered her as a pseudo *genius loci* (Susan Wood); statuettes from a cult of Jupiter Dolichenus, whose careful reinstallation in a shrine-like room in a late antique domus in Rome may indicate ongoing ritual significance, and not merely the intellectual pretensions of the homeowner (Blair Fowlkes-Child); an archaizing relief whose style and iconography echo the Palatine Campana plaques, but whose discovery at Nicopolis, the site founded by Augustus to commemorate his naval battle against Mark Antony, suggests connotations of military victory (Barbara Kellum). In all three cases, the artworks' ancient significance depended upon both their forms and their physical location. Had they surfaced on the art market, we would have missed the point completely.

The recent monograph by Jennifer Trimble on the so-called Large Herculaneum Woman thoroughly demonstrates both the method and the value of prioritizing grounded works over ungrounded ones. The widely replicated statue type was named after the specimen discovered in 1711 at the Theater of Herculaneum. In the book's second half, Trimble catalogs the 202 surviving replicas not according to typical rubrics—museum, state of preservation, iconography, or date—but rather by the province, region, and site of their discovery in the ground (Trimble 2011, 360–442). Those "with no provenance" appear in the final section of the catalog, and are omitted from the discussion in the book's main interpretive chapters (Trimble 2011, 442–5). So structured, the catalog foregrounds the users of these statues rather than their makers, thus offering a firm foundation for social art history. Building on the so-called "emulation" approach to Roman "copies" pioneered by scholars such as Elaine Gazda and Miranda Marvin, Trimble demonstrates how the meaning of the type shifts depending on each particular replica's location and social context (Marvin 1989; Gazda 1995 and 2002; Perry 2005; Marvin 2008; also Hallett 2005). In 23 CE, for example, a local patron at Puteoli honored Vipsania Agrippina (mother of Drusus, the recently deceased imperial heir) with a statue of this type. In this case, according to Trimble, the form embodied the notions of exemplary public femininity developed by Augustus to legitimize his dynastic ambitions, and "tied local actors into [the] distribution and legitimation" of "the claims of the ruling power" (Trimble 2011, 51). By contrast, at Sarmizegetusa, the capital of the newly conquered Roman province of Dacia, eight Large Herculaneum Woman statues "helped construct the inhabitants of Sarmizegetusa as behaviorally, socially, and culturally separate from the indigenous population" (Trimble 2011, 291).

The stars of Trimble's book reside in archaeological museums in Cherchel, Olympia, Antalya, Tulcea, and other far-flung locales. Among the pieces excluded from her analysis are some of the most beautiful examples, in the best-known collections, including the Louvre, the Hermitage, the Getty, and the Ny Carlsberg Glyptotek (as well as the one formerly in Boston that was featured on the cover of the *Nostoi* catalog). In a more traditionally conceived study, these specimens would likely have loomed largest (e.g. Andreae 2012, 39). Trimble's bold reversal of the field's typical methods and priorities will perhaps encourage other scholars to comb through the databases in new ways and seek out grounded specimens of the genres, types, or forms they are studying (additional studies that focus on grounded examples of widely replicated types to refine our understanding of their ancient social significance: Retzleff 2007; Kousser 2007).

The value of foregrounding context is particularly high in the classroom. Ideally, the objects held up as representative of "Roman Art" to newcomers to the field would be those with minimal modern repristination and maximal contextual data. Complete works (statues, herms, and busts) tell us more about Roman art and its significance than severed heads, and ensembles more than single works. Sometimes, this can be a matter of a simple substitution. Both the portrait of Menander found at Velia and that of a military hero from the theater at Cassino exhibit many of the "baroque," "pathos" qualities admired in the ungrounded portraits of Marius and Sulla in the Munich Glyptothek. The bronze head found near Chieti now in the Bibliothèque Nationale illustrates many of the same qualities the Capitoline Brutus is often used to demonstrate. The mother–daughter pair from Aphrodisias tells us much more about female self-fashioning in the Roman world than the Fonseca bust ever can; likewise the statues of Septimius and Julia Domna from the Perge Hydreion, compared to the busts in Indiana, and the reliefs from the Hypogeum of Yarhai compared to any of the lone Palmyrene reliefs that surfaced on the market. Likewise the ensemble of Aurelian and Severan imperial portraits discovered at Markouna, near Lambaesis in Algeria in 1851, compared to any single, ungrounded image of those rulers. But the value of these substitutions will only be realized with a more robust, conscious commitment to social art history. Currently, the leading textbooks (and, presumably, the courses that follow them) present the history of Roman art as a sequence of styles, with the odd observation about social significance grafted on here and there (Kleiner 1992 and 2010; Ramage and Ramage 2009; Andreae 2012). Even the textbooks organized around contexts (the domestic sphere, the funerary realm, cults, etc.) continue to feature ungrounded objects, whose original context can only be guessed at and discussed in the most general way (Elsner 1998; D'Ambra 1998; Stewart 2004; Schollmeyer 2005; Zanker 2008). Better use could be made of the well-preserved ensembles from the villa dei Papyri and the villas at Oplontis, Chiragan, and El Ruedo; from the sanctuary of Artemis Polo at Thasos, of Diana at Nemi, of Hercules Cubans in Trastevere, of Mars at Montmartre in Gallia Lugdunensis, the mithraeum at Sidon, the temple to the imperial cult at Misenum, the South Baths at Perge, the Nymphaeum of Herodes Atticus at Olympia, the theaters at Perge, Vaison-La-Romaine, and Butrint, the basilica at Velleia, the bouleu-terion at Aphrodisias, the Fora at Formia and Mérida, the tombs of the Haterii and of the Licinii at Rome, and of Yarhai at Palmyra, and the funerary monuments at Mainz, Aquileia, and Ostia. Sculpture in the Roman world featured in densely layered visual matrices that communicated specific messages about their patrons. The more of that complexity we can convey to students, the richer their understanding of the material will be.

Museums can also teach the public about the value of context, and not just the small, regional archaeological ones. Some recent reinstal-lations of prominent museum galleries are beginning to break the "masterpiece theater" pattern in favor of displaying ancient groups as groups. As noted in Chapter 5, the integrity of the ancient ensemble is beautifully preserved in the 1999 installation of the sculptures and reliefs from the Theater at Perge in a single, green-marble-veneered gallery at the Antalya Museum. Curators at the Ny Carlsberg Glyptotek relied on more subtle cues to mark out discrete ensembles within the museum's long, sculpture-filled, barrel-vaulted galleries, reorganized in 2006. Sculptures from Nemi, the Gardens of Sallust, and the ancient villa of Gaius Bruttius Praesens north of Rome, as well as the portraits from the Tomb of Licinii, are clustered together and face in toward one another. Similarly, the 2005 reorganization of the Conservatori wing of the Capitoline Museum displays the sculptural ensembles from the imperial *horti* together as discrete groups, with didactic maps and panels about the discoveries. Such installations encourage viewers to consider the individual objects in light not of other artworks deemed comparable by curators but rather alongside the works to which *ancient* users deemed them relevant.

An exceptionally far-ranging rethinking of installation priorities can now be seen in the new space devoted to works from the eastern Mediterranean under the Roman Empire at the Louvre, which opened in the fall of 2012. The objects in these galleries had previously been kept far apart from one another, divided among three separate curatorial departments largely on stylistic grounds (André-Salvini et al. 2012). They are now displayed in a unified suite of galleries that emphasizes the shared cultural horizons of Egypt and the Near East during the Roman period (Bel et al. 2012). A particularly vivid case study is the elegant arrangement of sculptures found in 1887 at the Mithraeum at Sidon (Bel 2012) (Fig. 18). The core of the ensemble is a group of seven marble statuettes with distinctively Mithraic iconography—Mithras slaying a bull, the Mithraic Kronos, and so on. Although Mithraism spread via the army throughout the Roman Empire, the cult had its origins in Iran. For this reason these sculptures fall under the domain of the Louvre's Department of Oriental Antiquities. The new display reunites them with a bronze figure of Aphrodite that was also apparently found at the site. She had parted company from her Mithraic associates at the moment of the Louvre's acquisition of the group in

Figure 18 Sculptures from a Mithraeum (now lost) in Sidon (Lebanon) in the newly-installed galleries devoted to the eastern Mediterranean under the Roman Empire at the Louvre. The site and its sculptures were discovered by the antiquarian Edmond Durighello. The sculptures passed through the hands of Louis Péretié, chancellor of the French consulate in Beirut, who sold them to the archaeology photographer Louis de Clercq. They were donated to the museum by his grandnephew, the Count H. de Boisgelin, in 1967. Note the bronze statuette of Aphrodite/Anahita on the left.

1967, when she was shunted off, on account of her Praxitelean forms, to the Department of Greek, Etruscan, and Roman Antiquities. Prior to the reinstallation of this wing of the museum, she had been displayed in the "Salle des Bronzes"—alongside works with which she shared nothing but her medium (Sophie Descamps, pers. com.). Restored to her Mithraic context, where she represents a conflation of Aphrodite and Anahita, mother of Mithra, this figure can now demonstrate the fluid syncretism of religion and visual culture in the Roman Empire. One hopes that the Louvre's context-centric model will be adopted elsewhere. Perhaps when the Istanbul Archaeological Museum reopens its Roman galleries, for example, the mother–daughter pair from Aphrodisias can be reunited with their late antique companions, including the older and younger chlamys-wearing office-holders and the Theodosian emperor.

The prioritization of context might also entail the repositioning of ungrounded, canonical works to a separate branch of the discipline—and a separate chapter of the textbook—devoted to the reception of Roman art. Objects such as the Fonseca bust, the Barberini Togatus, the Capitoline Brutus, the Marius and Sulla in Munich or the so-called Trebonianus Gallus in New York have much to tell us about the construction of an ideal classical past, the formation of taste, and the history of collecting, topics of growing scholarly interest. The bibliography on Grand Tourists, for example, and the market that developed to supply them, has expanded rapidly in recent years (Wilton and Bignamini 1996; Sicca and Yarrington 2000; Hornsby 2000; Scott 2003; Paul 2008; Coltman 2009; Bignamini and Hornsby 2010). There is much to learn from this literature. Bignamini has shown, for example, that far more so than today, a prestigious provenance enhanced the market value of ancient sculpture during the eighteenth century, a fact with many implications for scholars today (Bignamini and Hornsby 2010, xx–xxiv). One example is a bust of the emperor Septimius Severus, now in the Louvre, for which a findspot in the excavations at Herculaneum was claimed, despite the fact that Mt. Vesuvius buried Herculaneum more than a century prior to Septimius' reign (Ken Lapatin in Coates et al. 2012, 187).

The histories of particular collections have also attracted increasing attention in recent years (e.g. Carinci et al. 1990; Franceschini and Vernesi 2005; Fittschen 2006b; Christian 2010; Picozzi 2010; Aurenhammer and Sokolicek 2011; Auinger 2011). Some museums have begun telling those stories as part of their displays. The Antalya Museum has an extensive section devoted to the history of archaeology in the region, featuring a number of individual archaeologists and projects. One gallery in the Istanbul Archaeological Museum describes, through a series of text and photo panels, why and how objects such as the Alexander Sarcophagus and the reliefs from the Hecate Temple at Lagina were brought to the museum. Individual galleries on the second floor of the Villa Giulia Museum are devoted to particular antiquarian collections. Object labels and wall text reproduce eighteenth-century engravings of the pieces from the Athanasius Kircher collection and sales catalog pages from the Castellani firm, and discuss the ways in which the objects' importance and interpretation have shifted over time. At the Louvre, the grand Salle de Manège brings together, in the words of the large wall text facing the main entrance, "ancient sculpture from the great French and Italian collections restored in the 17th and 18th centuries." The foregrounding here of the sculptures' restoration, discussed and illustrated in rich detail in individual object labels, "permits the retracing of the history of interpretation" of ancient statuary. The gallery rightly celebrates the power of these artworks to teach us about early modern European history and visual culture, rather than that of the ancient world.

Itemize epistemological data

Students, scholars, collectors, and the general public alike will also pay more attention to questions of context if these are not obscured behind vague or ambiguous labels that elide findspot, ownership history, and hypotheses based upon style. All of this information, including second-hand dealers' reports, should be presented, but it must be clearly indicated for what it is. The new catalog of the Eastern Roman and Byzantine collections at the Louvre is exemplary in this regard, dedicating separate fields in the "tombstone" portion of its entries to findspot and ownership history, and presenting stylistic affinities in the analytical discussion below (Bel et al. 2012).

For both grounded and ungrounded objects, hypotheses about dates and identifications are strongest when supported by specific, grounded evidence. Here too, Trimble's recent book is a model. Not only does she carefully present the evidence for her proposed dates; she also explicitly differentiates among dates that are more and less secure. In addition to the main catalog organized by findspot, she provides a second, abbreviated catalog organized by time period (Trimble 2011, 351–9). Within each chronological division, the replicas are subdivided according to the quality of the evidence for the date. Category 1 objects have "firm dates," "established by analysis of a portrait head, fashion hairstyle, good associated epigraphic or archaeological evidence, the identification of the person portrayed, or multiple factors of these kinds that agree chronologically." Category 2 replicas can be assigned "good stylistic dates" through "close and convincing stylistic analysis" based on comparisons with objects in category 1. Specimens in category 3 can be assigned only "working dates," because they are "less firmly supported." Works in this category are "treated as meaningful evidence for larger chronological patterns and trends, but [Trimble has] tried to avoid relying on them as evidence of shorter-term developments." Category 4 works have "tentative, conflicting or disputed dates," and are excluded from final counts and summary charts.

The practices recommended here—the privileging of grounded works over ungrounded ones, the foregrounding of archaeological context, the full exposition of what is and is not known about the findspot and ownership history, the explicit discussion of the evidence and comparanda behind attributions—will no doubt make for longer books and articles, as Trimble's study amply demonstrates. That is a small price to pay for the increase in methodological transparency and epistemological clarity they will lend to the field. They will encourage students and scholars alike to think consciously about how we know what we think we know, and how we go from evidence to interpretation. They might even help to reduce looting, by fostering greater appreciation for the relative stability of grounded artworks, for the richness of our understanding of them and the complexity of the historical environments to which they belonged.

Bibliography

Ackerman, J. S. (1962), "A theory of style," *The Journal of Aesthetics and Art Criticism* 20 (3), 227–37.

—(1963), "The nature of art history" in J. S. Ackerman and R. Carpenter (eds), *Art and Archaeology*, New Jersey, 127–43.

Alexandridis, A. (2004), *Die Frauen des römischen Kaiserhauses. Eine Untersuchung ihrer bildlichen Darstellung von Livia bis Iulia Domna*, Mainz.

Alföldi, A. (1935), "Insignien und Tracht der römischen Kaiser," *Römische Mitteilungen* 50, 1–171.

Alpers, S. (1979), 'Style is what you make it: the visual arts once again' in B. Lang (ed.), *The Concept of Style*, Philadelphia, 95–117.

Amelung, W. (1903–8), *Die Sculpturen des Vaticanischen Museums*, Berlin.

Amy, R. and Seyrig, H. (1936), "Recherches dans la nécropole de Palmyre," *Syria* 17, 229–66.

Anderson, M. and Nista, L. (1988), *Roman Portraits in Context. Imperial and Private likenesses from the Museo Nazionale Romano*, Rome.

—(1989), *Radiance in Stone. Sculptures in Colored Marble from the Museo Nazionale Romano*, Rome.

Andreae, B. (2012), *L'Art Romain d'Auguste à Constantin*, Paris.

André-Salvini, B., Andreu-Lanoë, G., and Martinez, J.-L. (2012), "Avant-propos" in N. Bel et al., *L'Orient Romain et Byzantin au Louvre*, Paris.

di Apricena, M. B. (2000), "L'attività edilizia del vescovo Fonseca da Evora durante il XVIII Secolo" in M. B. di Apricena, *Il complesso dell'Aracoeli sul Colle Capitolino (IX–XIX secolo)*, Rome, 225–65.

Arata, F. P. (1994), "L'allestimento espositivo del Museo Capitolino al termine del pontificato di Clemente XII (1740)," *Bollettino dei musei comunali di Roma* 8, 45–94.

—(1996), "La nascita del Museo Capitolino" in M. E. Titoni (ed.), *Il Palazzo dei Conservatori e il Palazzo Nuovo in Campidoglio. Momenti di storia urbana di Roma*, Pisa, 75–81.

—(2008), "La diffusione e l'affermazione dei modelli artistici dell'antichità. Il ruolo del Museo Capitolino nella Roma del settecento" in A. D'Agliano and L. Melegati (eds), *Ricordi dell'Antico. Sculture, Porcellane e Arredi all'Epoca del Grand Tour*, Milan, 60–71.

Archaeological Institute of America, (2006), "Spinning a tale. Interview with Malcolm Bell," *Archaeology*, March 3.

Auinger, J. (2011), "The sculptural decoration of the Ephesian bath buildings in late antiquity" in O. Dally and C. Ratté (eds), *Archaeology and the Cities of Asia Minor in Late Antiquity*, Ann Arbor, 67–79.

Aurenhammer, M. and Sokolicek, A. (2011), "The remains of the centuries. Sculptures and statue bases in late antique Ephesus: the evidence of the upper agora" in O. Dally and C. Ratté (eds), *Archaeology and the Cities of Asia Minor in Late Antiquity*, Ann Arbor, 43–66.

Baharal, D. (1992), "The portraits of Julia Domna from the years 193–211 AD and the dynastic propaganda of L. Septimius Severus," *Latomus* 51, 110–18.

Balty, J. C. (1991), *Porträt und Gesellschaft in der römischen Welt*, Mainz.

Barbanera, M. (2010), "Dal testo all'immagine: autopsia delle antichità nella cultura antiquaria del settecento" in C. Brook and V. Curzi (eds), *Roma e l'antico. Realtà e visione nel'700*, Milan, 33–8.

Bardiès-Fronty, I., Walter, P. and Bimbenet-Privat, M. (2009), *Le Bain et le Miroir: Soins du Corps et Cosmétiques de l'Antiquité à la Renaissance*, Paris.

Barkan, E. (2002), "Amending historical injustices: the restitution of cultural property—an overview" in E. Barkan and R. Bush (eds), *Claiming the Stones/Naming the Bones: Cultural Property and the Negotiation of National and Ethnic Identity*, Los Angeles, 16–49.

Bartman, E. (1988), "*Decor et Duplicatio*: pendants on Roman sculptural display," *American Journal of Archaeology* 92, 211–25.

Bartman, E. (1991), "Sculptural collecting and display in the private realm" in E. Gazda (ed.), *Roman Art in the Private Sphere: New Perspectives on the Architecture and Decor of the Domus, Insula and Villa*, Ann Arbor, 71–88.

—(2001), "Hair and the artifice of Roman female adornment," *American Journal of Archaeology* 105, 1–25.

—(ed.), (2010), *La Lupa Capitolina: Nuove Prospettive di Studio*, Rome.

Bauer, A. A. (2008), "New ways of thinking about cultural property: a critical appraisal of the antiquities trade debate," *Fordham International Law Journal* 31, 690–724.

Bauer, A. A., Lindsay, S. and Urice, S. (2007), "When theory, practice and policy collide, or why do archaeologists support cultural property claims?" in Y. Hamilakis and P. Duke (eds), *Archaeology and Capitalism: From Ethics to Politics*, Walnut Creek, 45–58.

Bauer, H. (1986), "Form, Struktur, Stil: Die formalanalytischen und formgeschichtlichen Methoden" in H. Belting, H. Dilly, W. Kemp, W. Sauerländer and M. Warnke (eds), *Kunstgeschichte: Eine Einführung*, Berlin.

Beck, J. H. (1998), "Connoisseurship: A lost or a found art? The example of a Michelangelo attribution: 'The Fifth Avenue Cupid,'" *Artibus et Historiae* 37, 9–42.

—(2006), *From Duccio to Raphael. Connoisseurship in Crisis*, Florence.

Bel, N. (2012), "Les cultes à mystères Mithra" in N. Bel et al., *L'Orient Romain et Byzantin au Louvre*, Paris, 236–41.

Bel, N., Giroire, C., Gombert-Meurice, F. and Rutschowscaya, M.-H. (2012), *L'Orient Romain et Byzantin au Louvre*, Paris.

Bell, M. (1995), "The Motya Charioteer and Pindar's Isthmian 2," *Memoirs of the American Academy in Rome* 40, 1–42.

—(2011), "The Beautiful and the True," *Wall Street Journal*, July 2.

Bell, S. and Hansen, I. L. (eds) (2008), *Role Models in the Roman World. Identity and Assimilation*, Ann Arbor.

Belozerskaya, M. (2012), *Medusa's Gaze: the Extraordinary Journey of the Tazza Farnese*, Oxford.

Berenson, B. (1902), "Rudiments of connoisseurship" in B. Berenson, *The Study of Criticism of Italian Art*, London, 111–48.

Bergmann, B. (1994), "The Roman house as memory theater: the House of the Tragic Poet in Pompeii," *Art Bulletin* 76, 225–56.

—(1995), "Greek masterpieces and Roman recreative fictions," *Harvard Studies in Classical Philology* 97, 79–120.

—(2002), "Art and nature in the villa at Oplontis," *JRA* Suppl. 47, 87–120.

—(1977), "Studien zum römischen Porträt des 3. Jahrhunderts n. Chr.," *Antiquitas* 18, 19–22.

—(1999), *Chiragan, Aphrodisias, Konstantinopel: Zur mythologischen Skulptur der Spätantike*, Wiesbaden.

Bernoulli, J. J. (1882–94), *Römische Ikonographie*, 2 vols., Stuttgart.

Bertoletti, M., Cima, M. and Talamo, E. (1997), *Sculptures of Ancient Rome. Collections from the Capitoline Museums at the Montemartini Power Station*, Rome.

Bianchi, R. S. (2000), "On the nature of forgeries of ancient Egyptian works of art from the Amarna period," *Source* 20, 10–17.

Bianchi Bandinelli, R. (1967), "Arte plebea," *Dialoghi di Archeologia* 1, 7–19.

—(1970), *Rome: the Center of Power 500 B.C. to A.D. 200*, New York.

Bieber, M. (1977), *Ancient Copies: Contributions to the History of Greek and Roman Art*, New York.

Bignamini, I. and Claridge, A. (1998), "The tomb of Claudia Semne and excavations in eighteenth-century Rome," *Papers of the British School at Rome* 66, 215–44.

Bignamini, I. and Hornsby, C. (2010), *Digging and Dealing in Eighteenth-Century Rome*, New Haven and London.

Bisi, A. M. (1988), "La statua di Mozia nel quadro della scultura fenico-punica di ispirazione greca" in N. Bonacasa and A. Buttitta (eds), *La Statua Marmorea di Mozia*, Rome, 69–78.

Blümel, C. (1933), *Römische Bildnisse*, Berlin.

Boardman, J. (2006), "Archaeologists, collectors and museums" in E. Robson, L. Treadwell and C. Gosden (eds), *Who Owns Objects? The Ethics and Politics of Collecting Cultural Artefacts*, Oxford, 33–46.

Boatwright, M. T. (1993), "The city gate of Plancia Magna in Perge" in E. D'Ambra (ed.), *Roman Art in Context. An Anthology*, Upper Saddle River, 189–207.

Bol, R. (1984), *Das Statuenprogramm des Herodes-Atticus-Nymphäums*, Berlin.

Bonacasa, N. and Buttitta, A. (eds) (1988), *La Statua Marmorea di Mozia*, Rome.

Bonanno, A. (1988), "Imperial and private portraiture: a case of non-dependence" in N. Bonacasa and G. Rizza (eds), *Ritratto Ufficiale e Ritratto Privato: Atti del II Conferenza Internazionale sul Ritratto Romano*, Rome, Quaderni della ricerca scientifica 116, 157–64.

Borbein, A. H. (2000), "Formanalyse" in A. H. Borbein, T. Hölscher and P. Zanker (eds), *Klassische Archäologie. Eine Einführung*, Berlin, 109–28.

Borbein, A. H., Hölscher, T. and Zanker, P. (2000), "Einleitung" in A. H. Borbein, T. Hölscher and P. Zanker (eds), *Klassische Archäologie. Eine Einführung*, Berlin, 7–21.

Borg, B. (1996), *Mumienporträts: Chronologie und kultureller Kontext*, Mainz.

Born, H. and Stemmer, K. (1996), *Damnatio Memoriae: das Berliner Nero-Porträt*, Mainz.

Borzello, F. and Rees, A. L. (eds) (1986), *The New Art History*, London.

Boschung, D. (1986), "Überlegungen zum Liciniergrab," *Jahrbuch des Deutschen archäologischen Instituts* 101, 257–87.

—(2002), *Gens Augusta: Untersuchungen zu Aufstellung, Wirkung und Bedeutung der Statuengruppen des julisch-claudischen Kaiserhauses*, Mainz.

von Bothmer, D. (1981), "The death of Sarpedon" in S. L. Hyatt (ed.), *The Greek Vase: Papers based on lectures presented to a symposium held at Hudson Valley Community College at Troy, New York in April of 1979*, Latham, 63–80.

Bottari G. G. (1748), *Del Museo Capitolino 2, I Busti Imperiali*, Rome.

Bottini, A. and Setari, E. (eds) (2009), *Il Segreto di Marmo. I Marmi Dipinti di Ascoli Satriano*, Verona.

Brendel, O. J. (1979), *Prolegomena to the Study of Roman Art*, New Haven and London.

Brewer, J. (2009), *The American Leonardo: A Tale of Obsession, Art and Money*, Oxford.

Brodie, N., Kersel, M. M., Luke, C. and Tubb, K. W. (eds) (2006), *Archaeology, Cultural Heritage, and the Antiquities Trade*, Gainesville.

Brodie, N. and Tubb, K. W. (eds) (2002), *Illicit Antiquities: The Theft of Culture and the Extinction of Archaeology*, London and New York.

Brooks, R. (2005), *The Portland Vase: the Extraordinary Odyssey of a Mysterious Roman Treasure*, New York.

Buccino, L. (2011), "Morbidi capelli e acconciature sempre diverse, linee evolutive delle pettinature femminili nei ritratti scultorei dal secondo triumvirato all'età costantiniana" in E. La Rocca et al. (eds), *Ritratti. Le tante facce del potere*, Rome, 361–83.

Cadario, M. (2011), "Il linguaggio dei corpi nel ritratto romano" in E. La Rocca et al. (eds), *Ritratti. Le tante facce del potere*, Rome, 209–21.

Cagiano de Azevedo, E. (2008), *Rovine e Rinascite dell'Arte in Italia*, Milan.

Cameron, A. and Kuhrt, A. (eds) (1984), *Images of Women in Antiquity*, London.

Cappelli, R. (1992), *Bellezza e lusso. Immagini e documenti di piacere della vita*, Rome.

Carinci, F., Keutner, H., Musso, L. and Picozzi, M. G. (1990), *Catalogo della Galleria Colonna in Roma. Sculture*, Busto Arsizio.

Carruba, A. M. (2006), *La Lupa Capitolina: un Bronzo Medievale*, Rome.

Cartwright, L. and Sturken, M. (eds) (2001), *Practices of Looking: An Introduction to Visual Culture*, Oxford.

Cateni, G. (1998), *L'Ombra della Sera: Splendori Etruschi di Volterra*, Pisa.

Chastagnol, A. (1994), *Histoire Auguste*, Paris.

Chippindale, C. and Gill, D. W. J. (2000), "Material consequences of
   contemporary classical collecting," *American Journal of Archaeology* 104,
   463–511.

Christian, K. (2010), *Empire without End: Antiquities Collections in
   Renaissance Rome, c. 1350–1527*, New Haven and London.

Clark, T. J. (1974), "The conditions of artistic creation," *Times Literary
   Supplement*, May 24 [reprinted in E. Fernie (ed.) (1995), *Art History and
   Its Methods. A Critical Anthology*, London, 248–53].

Clarke, J. R. (1991), *The Houses of Roman Italy, 100 B.C.–A.D. 250: Ritual,
   Space, and Decoration*, Berkeley, Los Angeles and Oxford.

—(2003), *Art in the Lives of Ordinary Romans. Visual Representation and
   Non-Elite Viewers in Italy, 100 B.C.–A.D. 315*, Berkeley.

Clunas, C. (2003), "Social history of art" in R. S. Nelson and R. Shiff
   (eds), *Critical Terms for Art History*, 2nd edn, Chicago and London,
   465–77.

Coates, V. C. G., Lapatin, K. and Seydl, J. L. (eds) (2012), *The Last Days of
   Pompeii. Decadence, Apocalypse, Resurrection*, Los Angeles.

Coggins, C. C. (1969), "Illicit traffic of pre-Columbian antiquities," *Art
   Journal* 29, 94–8.

—(1998), "United States cultural property legislation: observations of a
   combatant," *International Journal of Cultural Property* 7, 52–68.

Cohen, B. (2010), "New light on a master bronze from Etruria," *American
   Journal of Archaeology* 114, online museum review.

Collins, J. (2010), "A nation of statues: museums and identity in eighteenth-
   century Rome" in D. A. Baxter and M. Martin (eds), *Architectural Space in
   Eighteenth-century Europe. Constructing Identities and Interiors*, Farnham,
   187–214.

Colonna, G. (2010), "Un monumento romano dell'inizio della Repubblica" in
   G. Bartoloni (ed.), *La Lupa Capitolina: Nuove Prospettive di Studio*, Rome,
   73–110.

Coltman, V. (2009), *Collecting Classical Sculpture in Britain since 1750*,
   Oxford.

Cooke, E. (2011), "What should we do with 'our' antiquities?," *Art Newspaper*
   229, November 17.

Corbett, D. P. (2005), "Visual culture and the history of art" in C. Van Eck
   and E. Winters (eds), *Dealing with the Visual: Art History, Aesthetics and
   Visual Culture*, Aldershot, 17–36.

Croz, J. F. (2002), *Les Portraits Sculptés de Romains en Grèce et en Italie de Cynosephales à Actium (197-31 av. J.C.)*, Paris.

Cuno, J. (2004), "The object of art museums" in J. Cuno (ed.), *Whose Muse? Art Museums and the Public Trust*, Princeton, 49–75.

—(2008), *Who Owns Antiquity? Museums and the Battle Over our Ancient Heritage*, Princeton and Oxford.

—(ed.) (2009), *Whose Culture? The Promise of Museums and the Debate Over Antiquities*, Princeton and Oxford.

D'Ambra, E. (1998), *Roman Art*, Cambridge and New York.

D'Ambra, E. and Métraux, G. P. R. (2006), *The Art of Citizens, Soldiers and Freedmen in the Roman World*, BAR International Series 1526, Oxford.

Dallas Museum of Art (n.d.), "Orpheus Taming Wild Animals." http://www.dallasmuseumofart.org/View/Deaccessions/deacc_6/deacc_6.

Daltrop, G. (1990), "Stèle funéraire de Gratidia M. L. Chrite et M. Gratidius Libanus" in J. Charles-Gaffiot and M. Albaric (eds), *Trésors du Vatican. La Papauté à Paris*, Paris, 192–3.

Davis, W. (1990), "Style and history in art history" in M. Conkey and C. Hastorf (eds), *The Uses of Style in Archaeology*, Cambridge, 18–31.

Davies, G. (2008), "Portrait statues as models for gender roles in Roman society" in S. Bell and I. L. Hansen (eds), *Role Models in the Roman World. Identity and Assimilation*, Ann Arbor, 207–20.

De la Bédoyère, G. (2006), *Roman Britain, A New History*, New York.

Delbrueck, R. (1912), *Antike Porträts*, Bonn.

—(1914), *Bildnisse römischer Kaiser*, Berlin.

Dillon, S. (1996), "The portraits of a civic benefactor of 2nd-century Ephesos," *Journal of Roman Archaeology* 9, 261–74.

—(2006), *Ancient Greek Portrait Sculpture. Contexts, Subjects, and Styles*, Cambridge and New York.

Dixon, S. (2001), *Reading Roman Women*, London.

Donohue, A. A. (2005), *Greek Sculpture and the Problem of Description*, Cambridge.

Dontas, G. (1988), "Un'opera siceliota, l'auriga di Mozia" in N. Bonacasa and A. Buttitta (eds), *La Statua Marmorea di Mozia*, Rome, 61–8.

Dorl-Klingenschmid, C. (2001), *Prunkbrunnen in kleinasiatischen Städten*, Munich.

Drerup, H. (1980), "Totenmaske und Ahnenbild bei den Römern," *Römische Mitteilungen* 87, 81–129.

Dyson, S. L. (1998), *Ancient Marbles to American Shores. Classical Archaeology in the United States*, Philadelphia.

—(2006), *In Pursuit of Ancient Pasts. A History of Classical Archaeology in the Nineteenth and Twentieth Centuries*, New Haven and London.

—(2012), "Museums and the market in antiquities," *Journal of Roman Archaeology* 25, 1004–7.

Eakin, H. (2006), "Must looted relics be ignored?," *New York Times*, May 2.

Eastlake, C. L. (1870), "How to observe" in C. L. Eastlake, *Contribution to the Literature of the Fine Arts*, London.

Ebitz, D. (1988), "Connoisseurship as practice," *Artibus et Historiae* 9, 207–12.

Edgers, G. (2011a), "Making Herakles whole after all these years," *The Boston Globe*, July 17.

—(2011b), "A detective's work at the MFA," *The Boston Globe*, December 11.

Elia, R. (1993), "A seductive and troubling work" [review of C. Renfrew, *The Cycladic Spirit: Masterpieces from the Nicholas P. Goulandris Collection*], *Archaeology* 46 (1), 64–9.

—(2009a), "Mythology of the antiquities market" in J. A. R. Nafziger and A. M. Nicgorski (eds), *Cultural Heritage Issues: The Legacy of Conquest, Colonization and Commerce*, Leiden, 239–55.

—(2009b), "Preventing looting through the return of looted archaeological objects," *Museum International* 61, 130–1.

Elsner, J. (1990), "Significant details: systems, certainties and the art historian as detective," *Antiquity* 64, 950–2.

—(1998), *Imperial Rome and Christian Triumph*, Oxford.

—(2003), "Style" in R. S. Nelson and R. Shiff (eds), *Critical Terms for Art History, Second Edition*, Chicago and London, 98–109.

—(2004), "Forward" [to the English translation of Hölscher 1987], Cambridge, xv–xxxi.

Erim, K. T. and Roueché, C. (1982), "Sculptors from Aphrodisias: some new inscriptions," *Papers of the British School at Rome* 50, 102–15.

Ewald B. (2003), "Sarcophagi and senators: the social history of Roman funerary art and its limits" [rev. of Wrede 2001], *Journal of Roman Archaeology* 16, 561–71.

Faedo, L. and Frangenberg, T. (2005), *Hieronymus Tetius. Aedes Barberinae ad Quirinalem descriptae. Descrizione di Palazzo Barberini al Quirinale. Il Palazzo, gli Affreschi, le Collezioni, la Corte*, Pisa.

Fejfer, J. (2008), *Roman Portraits in Context*, Berlin and New York.

Felch, J. and Frammolino, R. (2011), *Chasing Aphrodite. The Hunt for Looted Antiquities at the World's Richest Museum*, Boston and New York.

Ficoroni, F. de, (1744), *Le Vestigia e Rarità di Roma Antica*, Rome.

Fittschen, K. (1978), "Two portraits of Septimius Severus and Julia Domna," *Indiana University Art Museum Bulletin* 1 (2), 28–43.

—(1992–93), "Ritratti maschili privati di epoca adrianea: problemi della loro varietà," *Scienze dell'antichita: storia, archaeologia, antropologia* 6–7, 445–85.

—(1997), "Privatporträts hadrianischer Zeit" in J. Bouzek (ed.), *Roman Portraits, Artistic and Literary: Acts of the Third International Conference on Roman Portraits*, Prague, 32–6.

—(2006a), "Alte Bekannte. Zur Identifizierung verschollen geglaubter antiker Bildnisse," *Pegasus* 8, 169–94.

—(2006b) *Die Bildnisgalerie in Herrenhausen bei Hannover. Zur Rezeptions- und Sammlungsgeschichte Antiker Porträts*, Göttingen.

Fittschen, K. and Zanker, P. (1983), *Katalog der römischen Porträts in den Capitolinischen Museen und den anderen kommunalen Sammlungen der Stadt Rom, III: Kaiserinnen- und Prinzesinnenbildnisse: Frauenporträts*, Mainz.

—(1985), *Katalog der römischen Porträts in den Capitolinischen Museen und den anderen kommunalen Sammlungen der Stadt Rom, I: Kaiser- und Prinzenbildnisse*, Mainz.

Fitz Gerald, C. M. (1905), "Accessions by purchase. Bronze statue of Trebonianus Gallus," *Bulletin of the Metropolitan Museum of Art* 1, 12–13.

Flower, H. I. (1996), *Ancestor Masks and Aristocratic Power in Roman Culture*, Oxford.

Foçillon, H. (1934), *Vie des Formes*, Paris.

Foley, H. (ed.) (1981), *Reflections of Women in Antiquity*, London.

Fontanella, E. (2009), *Luxus. Il piacere della vita nella Roma imperiale*, Milan.

Formigli, E. (2010), "La storia della tecnologia dei grandi bronzi" in G. Bartoloni (ed.), *La Lupa Capitolina: Nuove Prospettive di Studio*, Rome, 15–24.

Formigli, E. (2012), "La Lupa Capitolina. Un antico monumento cade dal suo piedestallo e torna a nuova vita," *Römische Mitteilungen* 118.

Franceschini, M. and Vernesi, V. (eds) (2005), *Statue di Campidoglio. Diario di Alessandro Gregorio Capponi (1733-1746)*, Rome.

Friedländer, M. J. [1942] 1960, *On Art and Connoisseurship*, trans. T. Borenius, Boston.

Fuchs, W. (1988), "La statua marmorea di Mozia" in N. Bonacasa and A. Buttitta (eds), *La Statua Marmorea di Mozia*, Rome, 79–82.

Furtwängler, A. (1907), *Illustrierter Katalog der Glyptotek König Ludwig's I zu München*, Munich.

Gabucci, A. (2002), *Zenobia. Il Sogno di una Regina d'Oriente*, Milan.

Galinsky, K. (2008), "Recarved imperial portraits: nuances and wider context," *Memoirs of the American Academy in Rome* 52, 1–25.

Gaskell, I. (1996), "Writing and art history: against writing," *Art Bulletin* 78, 403–6.

Gasparri, C. and Guzzo, P. G. (2005), "Tomba o palazzo? Ipotesi funzionali per i marmi dipinti da Ascoli Satriano," *Rivista dell'Istituto Nazionale d'Archeologia e Storia dell'Arte* 60, 59-82.

Gatti, C. and Furiesi, A. (2011), *Alberto Giacometti e l'Ombra della Sera: dialogo tra due capolavori dall'arte etrusca al Novecento*, Milan.

Gazda, E. (1995), "Roman sculpture and the ethos of emulation: reconsidering repetition" in C. P. Jones, C. Segal, R. J. Tarrant and R. F. Thomas (eds), *Greece in Rome: Influence, Integration, Resistance*, Cambridge, 121–56.

—(2002), *The Ancient Art of Emulation: Studies in Artistic Originality and Tradition from the Present to Classical Antiquity*, Ann Arbor.

Gazda, E. and Haeckl, A. E. (1993), "Roman portraiture: reflections on the question of context," *Journal of Roman Archaeology* 6, 289–302.

George, M. (2005), "Family imagery and family values in Roman Italy" in M. George (ed.), *The Roman Family in the Empire: Rome, Italy and Beyond*, Oxford, 37–66.

Gerstenblith, P. (2003), "The McClain/Schultz doctrine: another step against trade in stolen antiquities," *Culture Without Context* 13 (Autumn). http://www.mcdonald.cam.ac.uk/projects/iarc/culturewithoutcontext/issue%2013/gerstenblith.htm

—(2006), "Recent developments in the legal protection of cultural heritage" in N. Brodie, M. M. Kersel, C. Luke and K. Walker-Tubb (eds), *Archaeology, Cultural Heritage, and the Antiquities Trade*, Gainesville, 69–92.

Ghedini, F. (1984), *Giulia Domna tra Oriente e Occidente. Le fonti archeologiche*, Rome.

Gibson-Wood, C. (1984), "Jonathan Richardson and the rationalization of connoisseurship," *Art History* 7, 38–56.

—(2000), *Jonathan Richardson. Art Theorist of the English Enlightenment*, London and New Haven.

Gill, D. W. J. (2009), "Looting matters for classical antiquities: contemporary issues in archaeological ethics," *Present Pasts* 1, 77–104.

Gill, D. W. J., Chippindale, C., Salter E. and Hamilton, C. (2001), "Collecting the classical world: first steps in a quantitative history," *International Journal of Cultural Property* 10, 1–31.

Ginzburg, C. (1980), "Morelli, Freud and Sherlock Holmes: clues and scientific method," *History Workshop* 9, 5–36.

Giordani, R. S. (1989), *Antichità Casali. La Collezione di Villa Casali a Roma*, Rome.

Giuliani, L. (1986), *Bildnis und Botschaft. Hermeneutische Untersuchungen zur Bildkunst der römischen Republik*, Berlin.

—(2000), "Antiken-Museen: Vergangenheit und Perspektiven einer Institution" in A. H. Borbein, T. Hölscher and P. Zanker (eds), *Klassische Archäologie. Eine Einführung*, Berlin, 77–90.

Godart, L. and de Caro, S. (2007), *Nostoi. Capolavori ritrovati*, Loreto.

Godau, S. (1989), "Inszenierung oder Rekonstruktion? Zur Darstellung von Geschichte im Museum" in M. Fehr and S. Grohe (eds), *Geschichte, Bild, Museum: Zur Darstellung von Geschichte im Museum*, Cologne, 199–211.

Goldhill, S. D. and Osborne, R. (1994), "Introduction: programmatics and polemics" in S. D. Goldhill and R. Osborne (eds), *Art and Text in Ancient Greek Culture*, Cambridge, 1–11.

Gombrich, E. (1950), *The Story of Art*, London.

—(1968), "Style" in D. Sills, *International Encyclopedia of the Social Sciences*, New York, 15:352-61.

Gopnik, B. (2012), "Who owns antiquity?" *Newsweek*, September 10.

Gosden, C. and Marshall, Y. (1999), "The cultural biography of objects," *World Archaeology* 31, 169–78.

Gourevitch, D. and Raepsaet-Charlier, M. T. (2003), *La Donna nella Roma Antica*, Firenze.

Greenberg, C. (1961), *Art and Culture: Critical Essays*, Boston.

Greenblatt, S. (1991), "Resonance and wonder" in I. Karp and S. D. Lavine (eds), *Exhibiting Cultures. The Poetics and Politics of Museum Display*, Washington, DC, 42–56.

Griffin, G. (1989), "Collecting Pre-Columbian art" in P. M. Messenger (ed.), *The Ethics of Collecting Cultural Property*, Albuquerque, 103–15.

Habinek, T. (1998), *The Politics of Latin Literature. Writing, Identity and Empire in Ancient Rome*, Princeton.

Hahn, H. (1946), *The Rape of La Belle*, Kansas City, MO.

Hales, S. and Hodos, T. (eds) (2010), *Material Culture and Social Identities in the Ancient World*, Cambridge and New York.

Hallett, C. (2005), "Emulation versus replication: redefining Roman copying," *Journal of Roman Archaeology* 16, 419–35.

Hamberg, P. G. (1945), *Studies in Roman Imperial Art, with Special Reference to the State Reliefs of the Second Century*, Uppsala.

Hannestad, N. (1994), *Tradition and Innovation in Late Antique Sculpture. Conservation, Modernization, Production*, Aarhus.

Hartswick, K. J. (2004), *The Gardens of Sallust. A Changing Landscape*, Austin.

Haskell, F. (1993), *History and its Images*, New Haven and London.

Hausmann, U. (1959), "Bildnisse zweier junger Römerinnen in Fiesole," *Jahrbuch des Deutschen archäologischen Instituts* 74, 164–202.

Helbig, W. (1891), *Führer durch die öffentlichen Sammlungen klassischer Altertümer in Rom*, Leipzig.

Herbert, J. D. (2003), "Visual culture/visual studies" in R. S. Nelson and R. Shiff (eds), *Critical Terms for Art History*, 2nd edn, Chicago and London, 452–64.

Hingley, R. (1990), *Roman Officers and English Gentlemen: the Imperial Origins of Roman Archaeology*, London.

Hofter, M. (1988), "Porträt" in M. Hofter (ed.), *Kaiser Augustus und die verlorene Republik: eine Ausstellung im Martin-Gropius-Bau*, Mainz, 291–343.

Hölscher, T. (1987), *Römische Bildsprache als semantisches System*, Heidelberg.

Hood, W. (1986), "In defense of Art History: a response to Brunilde Ridgway," *Art Bulletin* 68, 480–2.

Hornsby, C. (ed.), (2000), *The Impact of Italy: The Grand Tour and Beyond*, London.

Hoving, T. (1972), "Director's Note," *The Metropolitan Museum Bulletin of Art* 31, 1.

—(1996), *False Impressions. The Hunt for Big-Time Art Fakes*, New York.

Hülsen, C. (1913), "Die Grabgruppe eines römischen Ehepares im Vatikan," *Rheinisches Museum für Philologie* 68, 16–21.

Inan, J. and Alföldi-Rosenbaum, E. (1979), *Römische und frühbyzantinische Porträtplastik aus der Türkei. Neue Funde*, Mainz.

Jones, M. (ed.), (1990), *Fake? The Art of Deception*, London.

Joyce, R. A. (2012), "From place to place: provenience, provenance, and archaeology" in G. Feigenbaum and I. Reist (eds), *Provenance. An Alternate History of Art*, Los Angeles, 48–60.

Jucker, H. (1961), *Das Bildnis im Blätterkelch. Geschichte und Bedeutung einer römischen Porträtform*, Lausanne and Freiburg.

Kampen, N. B. (1981), *Image and Status: Roman Working Women in Ostia*, Berlin.

—(1997), "Democracy and debate: Otto Brendel's 'Prolegomena to a Book on Roman Art'", *Transactions of the American Philological Association* 127, 381–88.

Kennedy, R. and Eakin, H. (2006), "Met chief, unbowed, defends Museum's role," *New York Times*, February 28.

de Kersauson, K. (1996), *Catalogue des Portraits Romains, t. 11. De l'année de la guerre civile (68–69 ap. J.-C.) à la fin de l'empire*, Paris.

Kimmelman, M. (2006), "Is it all loot? Tackling the antiquities problem," *New York Times*, March 29.

Kinney, D. and Brilliant, R. (eds) (2011), *Reuse Value: Spolia and Appropriation in Art and Architecture from Constantine to Sherrie Levine*, Farnham, Surrey.

Kleiner, D. E. E. (1977), *Roman Group Portraiture: the Funerary Reliefs of the Late Republic and Early Empire*, New York.

—(1992), *Roman Sculpture*, New Haven and London.

—(2003), review of Wrede 2001, *American Journal of Archaeology* 107, 316–8.

Kleiner, D. E. E. and Matheson, S. B. (eds) (1996), *I, Claudia. Women in Ancient Rome*, Austin.

—(eds) (2000), *I, Claudia II. Women in Roman Art and Society*, Austin.

Kleiner, F. S. (1990), "On the publication of recent acquisitions of antiquities," *American Journal of Archaeology* 94, 525–7.

—(2010), *A History of Roman Art*, Belmont.

Koch, H. (1949), *Römische Kunst*, Weimar.

Kockel, V. (1993), *Porträtsreliefs stadtrömischer Grabbauten. Ein Beitrag zur Geschichte und zum Verständnis des spätrepublikanisch-frühkaiserzeitlichen Privatporträts*, Mainz.

Köhne, B. (1852), "Musée de sculpture antique de Mr. de Montferrand," *Zeitschrift für Münz-, Siegel- und Wappenkunde* 6, 1–97.

Koortbojian, M. (2007), "The double identity of Roman portrait statues: costumes and their symbolism" in J. Edmonson and A. Keith (eds), *Roman Dress and the Fabrics of Roman Culture*, Toronto, 71–93.

Kopytoff, I. (1986), "The cultural biography of things: commoditization as process" in A. Appadurai (ed.), *The Social Life of Things: Commodities in Cultural Perspective*, Cambridge, 64–91.

Kousser, R. (2007), "Mythological group portraits in Antonine Rome: the performance of myth," *American Journal of Archaeology* 111, 673–91.

Kragelund, P. (2002), "The emperors, the Licinii Crassi and the Carlsberg Pompey" in J. M. Høtje (ed.), *Images of Ancestors*, Aarhus, 185–222.

Kragelund, P., Moltesen, M. and Østergaard, J. S. (2003), *The Licinian Tomb. Fact or Fiction?* Copenhagen.

Kristeller, P. O. (1951; 1952), "The modern system of the arts", *Journal of the History of Ideas* 12, 496–527 and 13, 17–46.

Kruglov, A. V. (2010), "Late antique sculpture in Egypt: originals and forgeries" [review of Russmann 2009], *American Journal of Archaeology* 114, online museum review.

Kyrieleis, H. (2000), "Position des Deutschen Archäologischen Instituts" in M. Flashar (ed.), *Bewahren als Problem: Schutz archäologischer Kulturüter*, Freiburg, 163–6.

Lacayo, R. (2008), "Who owns history?," *Time*, February 21.

Lahusen, G. (1985), "Zur Funktion und Rezeption des römischen Ahnenbildes," *Römische Mitteilungen* 92, 261–89.

Lapatin, K. (2000), "Proof? The case of the Getty kouros," *Source* 20, 43–53.

La Regina, A. (2008), "La lupa del Campidoglio è medievale. La prova è nel test al carbonio," *La Repubblica*, July 9.

La Rocca, E. (2010), "Una questione di stile" in G. Bartoloni (ed.), *La Lupa Capitolina: Nuove Prospettive di Studio*, Rome, 117–50.

La Rocca, E., Presicce, C. P. and Lo Monaco, A. (2011), *Ritratti. Le Tante Facce del Potere*, Loreto.

—(2012), *L'Età dell'Equilibrio. Traiano, Adriano, Antonino Pio, Marco Aurelio*, Loreto.

Lavin, M. A. (1975), *Seventeenth-Century Barberini Documents and Inventories of Art*, New York.

Lenain, T. (2011), *Art Forgery. The History of a Modern Obsession*, Chippenham.

di Leo, B. (1989), "Alabaster" in M. Anderson and L. Nista (eds), *Radiance in Stone. Sculptures in Colored Marble from the Museo Nazionale Romano*, Rome, 52-4.

Longfellow, B. (2011), *Roman Imperialism and Civic Patronage. Form, Meaning and Ideology in Monumental Fountain Complexes*, Cambridge and New York.

Lopez, J. (2008), *The Man Who Made Vermeers. Unvarnishing the Legend of Master Forger Hans van Meegeren,* New York.

L'Orange, H. P. and von Gerkan, A. (1939), *Der spätantike Bildschmuck des Konstantinsbogen*, Berlin.

Lundén, S. (2004), "The scholar and the market. Swedish scholarly contributions to the destruction of the world's archaeological heritage" in H. Karlsson (ed.), *Swedish Archaeologists on Ethics*, Lindome, 197-247.

Lusnia, S. (forthcoming), *Creating Severan Rome: the Architecture and Self-Image of L. Septimius Severus (AD 193-211),* Brussels.

Lynes, R. (1968), "After hours. Forgery for fun and profit," *Harper's Magazine* 236, 21-8.

MacCormack, S. G. (1981), *Art and Ceremony in Late Antiquity*, Berkeley.

Mannsperger, M. (1998*), Frisurenkunst und Kunstfrisur: die Haarmode der römischen Kaiserinnen von Livia bis Sabina*, Bonn.

Mansel, A. M. (1975), "Die Nymphaen von Perge," *Istanbuler Mitteilungen* 25, 367-72.

Marcadé, J. (1996), *Sculptures Déliennes*, Paris.

Marchand, S. (1996), *Down from Olympus: archaeology and philhellenism in Germany, 1750-1970*, Princeton.

Marlowe, E. (2006), "Framing the sun: the Arch of Constantine and the Roman cityscape," *Art Bulletin* 88, 223-42.

—(forthcoming), "An unknown unknown. The so-called Trebonianus Gallus statue in New York" (manuscript under review).

Martini, M. (2010), "La datazione della terra di fusione" in G. Bartoloni (ed.), *La Lupa Capitolina: Nuove Prospettive di Studio*, Rome, 39-41.

Marvin, M. (1989), "Copying in Roman sculpture" in *Retaining the Original: Multiples Originals, Copies and Reproductions*, National Gallery Studies in the History of Art 20, Washington, 29-45.

—(2008), *The Language of the Muses. The Dialogue between Roman and Greek Sculpture*, Los Angeles.

Mastino, A. (2008), "Il dibattito sull'agora degli Italici a Delo: un bilancio retrospettivo fra ideologia e urbanistica" in S. Angiolillo, S. Boldrini and

P. Braconi (eds), *Le perle e il filo: a Mario Torelli per i suoi settanta anni*, Venosa, 233–41.

Mather, F. J., Jr. (1905), "A statue of Trebonianus Gallus," *Burlington Magazine* 8, 148–51.

Mayer, E. (2010), "Propaganda, staged applause or local politics? Public monuments from Augustus to Septimius Severus" in B. Ewald and C. Noreña (eds), *The Emperor and Rome: Space, Representation and Ritual*, Cambridge, 111–34.

—(2012), *The Ancient Middle Classes: Urban Life and Aesthetics in the Roman Empire, 100 BCE–250 CE*, Cambridge.

Mazzeo, R. (2005), "Patine su manufatti metallici," *Kermes Quaderni*, 29–43.

Mazzoni, C. (2010), *She-wolf. The Story of a Roman Icon*, Cambridge.

McCann, A. M. (1981), "Beyond the classical in third-century portraiture," *Aufstieg und Niedergang der römischen Welt* II.12.2., 623–45.

Mead, R. (2007), "Den of antiquity," *The New Yorker* 83, 52–61.

Megow, W.-R. (2005), *Republikanische Bildnis-Typen*, Frankfurt.

Melikian, S. (2012), "How UNESCO's 1970 Convention is weeding looted artifacts out of the antiquities market," *Art + Auction*, August 31.

Meyer, K. E. (1973), *The Plundered Past. The Story of the Illegal International Traffic in Works of Art*, New York.

Meyer, R. (2003), "Identity" in R. S. Nelson and R. Shiff, *Critical Terms for Art History*, 2nd edition, Chicago and London, 345–57.

Michael C. Carlos Museum, (2011), *Highlights of the Collection*, Atlanta.

Mickocki, T. (1995), *Sub Specie Deae. Les Impératrices et princesses romaines assimilées à des déesses*, Rome.

Minor, H. H. (2010), *The Culture of Architecture in Enlightenment Rome*, University Park.

Molholt, R. (2011), "Roman labyrinth mosaics and the experience of motion," *Art Bulletin* 93, 287–303.

Moltesen, M. (1997), *In the Sacred Grove of Diana*, Copenhagen.

Moltesen, M. (2000), "The Esquiline group. Aphrodisian statues in the Ny Carlsberg Glyptotek," *Antike Plastik* 27, 111–29.

de Montebello, P. (2009), "And what do you suppose should be done with those objects?" in J. Cuno (ed.), *Whose Culture? The Promise of Museums and the Debate Over Antiquities*, Princeton and Oxford, 55–70.

Moon, W. G. (ed.) (1995), *Polykleitos, the Doryphoros and Tradition*, Madison.

Moralee, J. (2008), "Maximinus Thrax and the politics of race in late antiquity," *Greece & Rome* 55, 55–82.

Morelli, G. (1890), "Princip und Methode" in G. Morelli, *Kunstkritische Studien über italienische Malerei. Die Galerien Borghese und Doria Panfili in Rom*, Leipzig, 1–63.

—(1892–3), *Italian Painters: Critical Studies of their Works*, London.

Murr, A. (2008), "Murky provenance," *Newsweek*, January 24.

Muscarella, O. W. (1984), "On publishing unexcavated artifacts," *Journal of Field Archaeology* 11, 61–6.

—(2000), *The Lie Became Great. The Forgery of Near Eastern Cultures*, Groningen.

—(2009), "The fifth column within the archaeological realm: the great divide" in Z. Derin, H. Saglamtinmur and E. Abay (eds), *Studies in Honour of Altan Çilingiroğlu: A Life Dedicated to Urartu on the Shores of the Upper Sea*, Istanbul, 395–406.

Neer, R. T. (2005), "Connoisseurship and the stakes of style," *Critical Inquiry* 32, 1–26.

Newhouse, V. (2005), *Art and the Power of Placement*, New York.

Niemeyer, H. G. (1968), *Studien zur statuarischen Darstellung der römischen Kaiser*, Berlin.

Nodelman, S. (1982), "A portrait of the Empress Plautilla," *J. Paul Getty Museum Journal* 10, 105–20.

Norman, N. J. (2005), "Editorial policy on the publication of recently acquired antiquities," *American Journal of Archaeology* 109, 135–6.

de Nuccio, M. and Ungaro, L. (2002), *I Marmi Colorati della Roma Imperiale*, Venice.

Oakley, J. H. (1998), "Why study a Greek vase-painter? A response to Whitley's 'Beazley as theorist,' " *Antiquity* 72, 209–13.

Olin, M. (1994), "Violating the second commandment's taboo: why art historian Meyer Schapiro took on Bernard Berenson," *Forward*, November 4, 23.

Osborne, R. (2010), "The art of signing in ancient Greece" in V. Platt and M. Squire (eds), *The Art of Art History in Greco-Roman Antiquity* (special edition of *Arethusa*, 43 (2)), 231–51.

Owen, D. I. (2009), "Censoring knowledge: the case for the publication of unprovenanced cuneiform tablets" in J. Cuno (ed.), *Whose Culture? The Promise of Museums and the Debate over Antiquities*, Princeton and Oxford, 125–42.

Özgür, M. E. (2008), *Sculptures of the Museum in Antalya*, Ankara.

Palagia, O. and Pollitt, J. J. (eds), (1996), *Personal Styles in Greek Sculpture*, Cambridge and New York.

Pappalardo, U. (1997), "Nuove testimonianze su Marco Nonio Balbo ad Ercolano," *Römische Mitteilungen* 104, 417–33.

—(2005), "Marcus Nonius Balbus. Der Patronus von Herculaneum" in J. Mühlenbrock and D. Richter, *Verschüttet vom Vesuv. Die letzten Studen von Herculaneum*, Berlin, 171–81.

Parlasca, K. (1969–80), *Ritratti di mumie. Repertorio d'art dell'Egitto greco-romano*, Rome.

—(2000), "Eine neue Monographie über Mumienbildnisse," *Chronique d'Égypte* 75, 171–86.

Paul, C. (2007), "The Capitoline Hill and the birth of the modern museum" in J. Luckhardt and M. Wiemers (eds), *Museen und fürstliche Sammlungen im 18. Jahrhundert. Museums and Princely Collections in the 18th Century*, Braunschweig, 66–72.

—(2008), *The Borghese Collections and the Display of Art in the Age of the Grand Tour*, Aldershot.

—(2012), "Capitoline Museum, Rome: civic identity and personal cultivation" in C. Paul (ed.), *The First Modern Museums of Art. The Birth of an Institution in 18th- and Early-19th Century Europe*, Los Angeles, 21–45.

Pedley, J. G. (1997), "Provenience: 'unknown,'" *Journal of Roman Archaeology* 10, 604–9.

Perry, E. (2005), *The Aesthetics of Emulation in the Visual Arts of Ancient Rome*, Cambridge.

Petersen, L. H. (2006), *The Freedman in Roman Art and Art History*, Cambridge.

Picón, C. A., Mertens, J. R., Milleker, E. J., Hemingway, S. and Lightfoot, C. (2007), *Art of the Classical World in the Metropolitan Museum of Art. Greece, Cyprus, Etruria, Rome*, New Haven and London.

Picozzi, M. G. (2010), "Le sculture degli appartamenti. Contributo alla storia delle antichità della famiglia Colonna" in M. G. Picozzi, *Palazzo Colonna. Appartamenti, Sculture antiche e dall'antico*, Rome, 11–84.

Pietrangeli, C. (1982), *The Vatican Collections. The Papacy and Art*, New York.

Pinelli, O. R. (2010), "Winckelmann e la storiografia artistica nella seconda metà del Settecento" in C. Brook and V. Curzi (eds), *Roma e l'antico. Realtà e visione nel'700*, Milan, 45–50.

Pinotti, A. (2012), "Formalism and the history of style" in M. Rampley et al. (eds), *Art History and Visual Studies in Europe. Transnational Discourses and National Frameworks*, Leiden and Boston, 75–90.

Platt, V. and Squire, M. (eds) (2010), *The Art of Art History in Graeco-Roman Antiquity* (special edition of *Arethusa*, 43 (2)).

Podro, M. (1982), *The Critical Historians of Art*, New Haven and London.

Pollini, J. (2007), "Ritualizing death in Republican Rome. Memory, religion, class struggle and the wax ancestral mask tradition's origin and influence on veristic portraiture" in N. Lanera (ed.), *Performing Death. Social Analyses of Funerary Traditions in the Ancient Near East and Mediterranean*, Chicago, 237–85.

Pomeroy, S. B. (1975), *Goddesses, Whores, Wives and Slaves: Women in Classical Antiquity*, New York.

Presicce, C. P. (2010a), "Nascita e fortuna del Museo Capitolino" in C. Brook and V. Curzi (eds), *Roma e l'antico. Realtà e visione nel'700*, Milan, 91–8.

—(2010b), "I Musei Capitolini. Cenni storici" in E. La Rocca and C. P. Presicce (eds), *Musei Capitolini. Le Sculture del Palazzo Nuovo*, Milan, 17–29.

Price, S. (1984), *Rituals and Power: the Roman Imperial Cult in Asia Minor*, Cambridge.

Raeder, J. (1992), "Herrscherbildnis und Münzpropaganda. Zur Deutung des 'Serapistypus' des Septimius Severus," *Jahrbuch des Deutschen Archäologischen Instituts* 107, 175–96.

Rauh, N. K. (1993), *The Sacred Bonds of Commerce: Religion, Economy and Trade Society at Hellenistic Roman Delos, 166–87 B.C.*, Amsterdam.

Ramage, N. H. and Ramage, A. (1991) *Roman Art. Romulus to Constantine*, 1st edition, Upper Saddle River.

—(2009), *Roman Art. Romulus to Constantine*, 5th edition, Upper Saddle River.

Renfrew, C. (1993), "Collectors are the real looters," *Archaeology* 46 (3), 16–17.

—(2000), *Loot, Legitimacy and Ownership*, London.

—(2010), "Combating the illicit antiquities trade: progress and problems," *Newsletter Ufficio Studi* 2, 9–13.

Retzleff, A. (2007), "The Dresden type Satyr-Hermaphrodite group in Roman theaters," *American Journal of Archaeology* 111, 459–72.

Reusser, C. (2002), *Vasen fur Etrurien: Verbreitung und Funktionen attischer Keramik im Etrurien des 6. und 5. Jahrhunderts v. Chr.*, Zurich.

Richardson, J. (1719), *Two Discourses. I. The Connoisseur: an Essay on the Whole Art of Criticism as it Relates to Painting. II. An Argument in Behalf of the Science of a Connoisseur: Wherein is Shewn the Dignity, Certainty, Pleasure and Advantage of it*, London.

Richardson, L., Jr. (2000), *A Catalog of Identifiable Figure Painters of Ancient Pompeii, Herculaneum and Stabiae*, Baltimore.

Richter, G. M. A. (1915), *Greek, Etruscan and Roman Bronzes*, New York.

Ridgway, B. S. (1986), "The state of research on ancient art," *Art Bulletin* 68, 7–23.

—(1994), "The study of classical sculpture at the end of the twentieth century," *American Journal of Archaeology* 98, 759–72.

—(2005), "The study of Greek sculpture in the twenty-first century," *Proceedings of the American Philosophical Society* 149, 63–71.

Riegl, A. (1901), *Spätrömische Kunstindustrie*, Vienna.

Riggs, C. (2002), "Facing the dead: recent research on the funerary art of Ptolemaic and Roman Egypt," *American Journal of Archaeology* 106, 85–101.

Rodenwaldt, G. (1935), *Über den Stilwandel in der antoninischen Kunst*, Berlin.

Rose, C. B. (1997), *Dynastic Commemoration and Imperial Portraiture in the Julio-Claudian Period*, Cambridge.

—(2008), "Forging identity in the Roman Republic: Trojan ancestry and veristic portraiture" in S. Bell and I. L. Hansen (eds), *Role Models in the Roman World. Identity and Assimilation*, Ann Arbor, 97–131.

Russmann, E. R. (2009), *Unearthing the Truth. Egypt's Pagan and Coptic Sculpture*, New York.

Scallen, C. B. (2004), *Rembrandt, Reputation and the Practice of Connoisseurship*, Amsterdam.

Schapiro, M. (1953), "Style" in A. L. Krober (ed.), *Anthropology Today: An Encyclopedic Inventory*, Chicago, 287–312 (reprinted in M. Schapiro, 1994, *Theory and Philosophy of Art: Style, Artist, and Society*, New York, 51–102).

—(1961), "Mr. Berenson's values," *Encounter* 16, 57–65 (reprinted in M. Schapiro, 1994, *Theory and Philosophy of Art: Style, Artist, and Society*, New York, 209–26).

Schiffer, M. B. and Miller, A. (1999), *The Material Life of Human Beings: Artifacts, Behavior and Communication*, London.

Schmidt-Colinet, A. (1991), "Eine severische Priesterin aus Syrien in Perge," *Istanbuler Mitteilungen* 41, 439–45.

Schmidt-Colinet., A. et al. (1992), *Das Tempelgrab Nr. 36 in Palmyra. Studien zur palmyrenischen Grabarchitektur und ihrer Ausstatung*, Mainz.

Schollmeyer, P. (2005), *Römische Plastik. Ein Einführung*, Darmstadt.

Schröter, E. (1993), "Der Kolossalkopf 'Alexanders des Großen' im Cortile della Pigna und andere Antiken der Villa Mattei im Vatikan," *Pantheon* 51, 101–28.

Schwartz, G. (1995), "Rembrandt research after the age of connoisseurship," *Annals of Scholarship* 10, 313–35.

Scott, J. (2003), *The Pleasures of Antiquity: British Collectors of Greece and Rome*, New Haven and London.

Scott, S. (2003), "Provincial art and Roman imperialism: an overview" in S. Scott and J. Webster (eds), *Roman Imperialism and Provincial Art*, Cambridge, 1–7.

—(2006), "Art and the archaeologist," *World Archaeology* 38, 628–43.

Scott, S. and Webster, J. (eds) (2003), *Roman Imperialism and Provincial Art*, Cambridge.

Shanks, M. (1996), *Classical Archaeology of Greece: Experiences of the Discipline*, London.

Shirey, D. (1973), "Von Bothmer quits Archaeology unit," *New York Times*, May 2.

Sicca, C. and Yarrington, A. (eds) (2000), *The Lustrous Trade. Material Culture and the History of Sculpture in England and Italy, 1700–1860*, London.

Silver, V. (2009), *The Lost Chalice. The Epic Hunt for a Priceless Masterpiece*, New York.

Simpson, C. (1986), *Artful Partners. Bernard Berenson and Joseph Duveen*, New York.

Smith, R. R. R. (1988a), *Hellenistic Royal Portraits*, Oxford and New York.

—(1988b), Review of Luca Giuliani (1986), "*Gnomon*" 60, 7613–6.

—(1998), "Cultural choice and political identity in honorific portrait statues in the Greek East in the second century A.D.," *Journal of Roman Studies* 88, 56–93.

—(1999), "Late antique portraits in a public context: honorific statuary at Aphrodisias in Caria, AD 300–600," *Journal of Roman Studies* 89, 155–89.

—(2002a), "The use of images: visual history and ancient history" in T. P. Wiseman (ed.), *Classics in Progress. Essays on Ancient Greece and Rome*, Oxford, 59–102.

—(2002b), "The statue monument of Oecumenius: a new portrait of a late antique governor from Aphrodisias," *Journal of Roman Studies* 92, 134–56.

—(2007), "Statue life in the Hadrianic Baths at Aphrodisias, AD 100–600: local context and historical meaning" in F. A. Bauer and C. Witschel (eds), *Statuen in der Spätantike,* Wiesbaden, 203–35.

Smith, R. R. R., Dillon, S., Hallett, C. H., Lenaghan, J. and van Voorhis, J. (eds) (2006), *Roman Portrait Statuary from Aphrodisias,* Mainz.

Spanel, D. (2001), "Two groups of 'Coptic' sculpture and relief in the Brooklyn Museum of Art," *Journal of the American Research Center in Egypt* 38, 89–113.

Spencer, R. D. (2004a), " 'The authentic will win out.' Eugene Victor Thaw interviewed by Ronald D. Spencer" in R. D. Spencer (ed.), *The Expert Versus the Object. Judging Fakes and False Attributions in the Visual Arts,* Oxford, 73–7.

—(ed.) (2004b), *The Expert Versus the Object. Judging Fakes and False Attributions in the Visual Arts,* Oxford.

Spinola, G. (1999), *Il Museo Pio Clementino* 2, Vatican City.

Spivey, N. and Rasmussen, T. (eds) (1991), *Looking at Greek Vases,* Cambridge.

Squire, M. (2009), *Image and Text in Graeco-Roman Antiquity,* Cambridge and New York.

—(2012), "Classical Archaeology and the Contexts of Art History" in S. Alcock and R. Osborne (eds), *Classical Archaeology,* 2nd edition, Malden, 468–93.

Stephens, J. (2008), "Ancient Roman hairdressing: on (hair)pins and needles," *Journal of Roman Archaeology* 21, 111–32.

Stewart, P. (2003), *Statues in Roman Society. Representation and Response,* Oxford.

—(2004), *Roman Art,* Oxford.

—(2008), *The Social History of Roman Art,* Cambridge.

Stirling, L, (2005), *The Learned Collector. Mythological Statuettes and Classical Taste in Late Antique Gaul,* Ann Arbor.

Stray, C. (1998), *Classics Transformed: Schools, Universities, and Society in England, 1830–1960,* Oxford.

Strong, E. S. (1907), *Roman Sculpture from Augustus to Constantine,* London.

Stuart Jones, H. (1912), *A Catalogue of the Ancient Sculptures Preserved in the Municipal Collections of Rome. The Sculptures of the Museo Capitolino,* Oxford.

Sutton, P. C. (2007), "Introduction" in P. C. Sutton, N. Hall-Duncan, A. D. Newman, and J. Martin (eds), *Fakes and Forgeries: the Art of Deception*, Greenwich, 13–25.

Sutton, P. C., Hall-Duncan, N., Newman, A. D. and Martin, J. (eds) (2007), *Fakes and Forgeries: the Art of Deception*, Greenwich.

Talley, M. K., Jr. (1989), "Connoisseurship and the methodology of the Rembrandt Research Project," *International Journal of Museum Management and Curatorship* 8, 175–214.

Tancock, J. L. (2004), "Issues of authenticity in the auction house" in R. D. Spencer (ed.), *The Expert Versus the Object. Judging Fakes and False Attributions in the Visual Arts*, Oxford, 45–53.

Technau, W. (1940), *Die Kunst der Römer*, Berlin.

Thomson, M. (2012), *Studies in the Historia Augusta*, Brussels.

Tomei, M. A. (1999), *Scavi Francesi sul Palatino. Le Indagini di Pietro Rosa per Napoleone III (1861–1870)*, Rome.

Trillmich, W. (1974), "Ein Bildnis der Agrippina Minor von Milreu/Portugal," *Madrider Mitteilungen* 15, 184–202.

Trimble, J. (2011), *Women and Visual Replication in Roman Imperial Art and Culture*, Cambridge.

Trümper, M. (2008), *Die 'Agora des Italiens' in Delos: Baugeschichte, Architektur, Ausstattung und Funktion einer späthellenistischen Porticus-Anlage*, Rahden/Westf.

Turner, F. (1981), *The Greek Heritage in Victorian Britain*, New Haven and London.

Tyszkiewicz, M. (1898), *Memories of an Old Collector*, London, New York, and Bombay.

van de Wetering, E. (2001), "Thirty years of the RRP: the tension between science and connoisseurship in authenticating art," *International Foundation for Art Research Journal* 4 (2), 14–24.

—(2005), *A Corpus of Rembrandt Paintings IV: The Self-Portraits*, Dordrecht.

—(2008), "Connoisseurship and Rembrandt's paintings: new directions in the Rembrandt Research Project, part II," *The Burlington Magazine* 150, 83–90.

van Keuren, F. (2003), "Unpublished documents shed new light on the Licinian Tomb, discovered in 1884–1885, Rome," *Memoirs of the American Academy in Rome* 48, 53–139.

Varner, E. (2004), *Mutilation and Transformation: Damnatio Memoriae and Roman Imperial Portraiture*, Leiden and Boston.

Venetucci, B. P. (1998), *Pirro Ligorio e le Erme di Roma*, Rome.

Vermeule, C. C. (1981), *Greek and Roman Sculpture in America. Masterpieces in Public Collections in the United States and Canada*, Berkeley and Los Angeles.

Vessberg, O. (1941), *Studien zur Kunstgeschichte der römischen Republik*, Lund.

Vickers, M. and Gill, D. W. J. (1994), *Artful Crafts: Ancient Greek Silverware and Pottery*, Oxford.

Visconti, E. Q. (1807), *Il Museo Pio Clementino VII*, Milan.

di Vita, A. (1988), "La statua di Mozia" in N. Bonacasa and A. Buttitta (eds), *La Statua Marmorea di Mozia*, Rome, 39–52.

Vogel, S. (1991), "Always true to the object, in our fashion" in I. Karp and S. D. Levine (eds), *Exhibiting Cultures: the Poetics and Politics of Museum Display*, Washington and London, 191–204.

Volpi, F. (1986–87), "Rilievi funerari urbani con busti-ritratto," *Annali della Facoltà di lettere e filosofia, Università di Perugia* 24, 243–304.

Vout, C. (2012), "Putting the art into artefact" in S. Alcock and R. Osborne (eds), *Classical Archaeology*, 2nd edition, Malden, 442–67.

Vrdoljak, A. F. (2006), *International Law, Museums and the Return of Cultural Objects*, Cambridge.

Walker, S. (2000), *Ancient Faces: Mummy Portraits from Roman Egypt*, New York.

Wallace-Hadrill, A. (1994*), Houses and Society in Pompeii and Herculaneum*, Princeton.

Warden, P. G. (2011), "The Chimaera of Arezzo: made in Etruria?", *American Journal of Archaeology* 115, 1–5.

Warden, P. G. and Romano, D. (1994), "The course of glory: Greek art in Roman context at the Villa of the Papyri at Herculaneum," *Art History* 17, 228–54.

Watson, P. and Todeschini, C. (2006), *The Medici Conspiracy. The Illicit Journey of Looted Antiquities from Italy's Tomb Raiders to the World's Greatest Museums*, New York.

Watt, J. C. Y. (2009), "Antiquities and the importance—and limitations—of archaeological contexts" in J. Cuno (ed.), *Whose Culture? The Promise of Museums and the Debate Over Antiquities*, Princeton and Oxford, 89–106.

Waxman, S. (2008a), *Loot: The Battle Over the Stolen Treasures of the Ancient World*, New York.

—(2008b), "How did that vase wind up in the Metropolitan?", *New York Times*, December 1.

Weitzmann, K. (ed.), (1979), *Age of Spirituality. Late Antique and Early Christian Art, Third to Seventh Century*, New York.

White, S. (2005), "Building American museums. The role of the private collector" in K. Fitz Gibbon (ed.), *Who Owns the Past? Cultural Policy, Cultural Property and the Law*, New Brunswick and London, 165–77.

Whitley, A. J. (1997), "Beazley as theorist," *Antiquity* 71, 40–7.

—(2001), *The Archaeology of Ancient Greece*, Cambridge.

Wickhoff, F. (1895), *Die Wiener Genesis*, Vienna.

Wilton, A. and Bignamini, I. (eds) (1996), *The Grand Tour: The Lure of Italy in the Eighteenth Century*, London.

Winter, B. W. (2003), *Roman Wives, Roman Widows. The Appearance of New Women and the Pauline Communities*, Grand Rapids.

Wiseman, J. (1984), "Scholarship and provenience in the study of artifacts," *Journal of Field Archaeology* 11, 67–77.

Woelk, M. (2007), "From the menagerie to the plaster gallery: the Herculaneum Women in Dresden" in J. Daehner (ed.), *The Herculaneum Women. History, Context, Identities*, Los Angeles.

Wölfflin, H. (1899), *Klassische Kunst*, Munich.

Wood, S. (1999), *Imperial Women: a Study in Public Images 40 B.C.–A.D. 68*, Leiden.

Wrede, H. (1971), "Das Mausoleum der Claudia Semne und die bürgerliche Plastik der Kaiserzeit," *Römische Mitteilungen* 78, 125–66.

—(2001), *Senatorische Sarkophage Roms. Der Beitrag des Senatorenstandes zur römischen Kunst der hohen und späten Kaiserzeit*, Mainz.

Zadoks-Josephus Jitta, A. N. (1932), *Ancestral Portraiture in Rome and the Art of the Last of the Republic*, Amsterdam.

Zanker, P. (1975), "Grabreliefs römischer Freigelassener," *Jahrbuch des deutschen archäologischen Instituts* 90, 267–315.

—(1983), "Zur Bildnisrepräsentation führender Männer in mittelitalischen und campanischen Städten zur Zeit der späten Republik und der julisch-claudischen Kaiser" in M. Cébeillac-Gervasoni (ed.), *Les "Bourgeoisies" municipales italiennes aux IIe et Ier siècles av. J.-C.*, Paris, 251–66.

—(1988), *The Power of Images in the Age of Augustus*, Ann Arbor.

—(1989), "Statuenrepräsentation und Mode" in S. Walker and A. Cameron (eds), *The Greek Renaissance in the Roman Empire: Papers from the Tenth British Museum Classical Colloquium*, London, 102–7.

—(1995), "Individuum und Typus. Zur Bedeutung des realistischen Individualporträts der späten Republik," *Archäologischer Anzeiger* 95, 473–81.

—(1999), *Pompeii: Public and Private Life*, Cambridge, MA.

—(2008), *Arte Romana*, Rome-Bari.

—(2011), "Individuo e tipo. Riflessioni sui ritratti individuali realistici nella tarda Repubblica" in E. La Rocca et al. (eds), *Ritratti. Le tante facce del potere*, Rome, 109–19.

Zevi, C. B. C. and Restellini, M. (eds) (2011), *Giacometti et les Étrusques*, Prato.

Zimmer, G. (1982), *Römische Berufsdarstellungen. Archäologische Forschungen* 12, Berlin.

Index of artworks and monuments

Page references in italics denote a figure.

Index

Page numbers in italics denote a figure.